The Patriots Handbook

Beverly A. Potter

Ronin Publishing, Inc
Berkeley, California

The Patriots Handbook

Copyright 2010: Beverly A. Potter
ISBN: 978-1-57951-108-1

Published by
Ronin Publishing, Inc.
PO Box 22900
Oakland, CA 94609
www.roninpub.com

All rights reserved. No part of this work may be reproduced or transmitted in any form by any means electronic or mechanical, including photocopying recording or translating into another language, or by any information storage or retrieval system, without written permission from the author or the publisher, except for inclusion of brief quotations in a review.

Library of Congress Card Number: 2010910760
Distributed to the book trade by PGW/Perseus

Credits:
Material in Forms of Government (Chapter 8), The Executive Branch (Chapter 11), The Supreme Court (Chapter 12) and The Legislative Branch (Chapter 13) was excerpted from material prepared by the U.S. Government Printing Office. Banners with presidential images were prepared by the U.S. Government Printing Office. Where Do You Stand Politically? (Chapter 15) is based on the work of David Nolan and copyright is held by Advocates for Self Government. Who Determines Constitutionality? (Chapter 21) was authored by Brian Roberts and copyright 2010 is held by TenthAmendmentCenter.com. The Tenth Amendment (Chapter 22) is copyright 2010 and held by TenthAmendmentCenter. com. The Amendment to Repeal the 17th Amendment (page 155) was authored by John Macmullin.

The Patriots Handbook

Beverly A. Potter

Other Books by Beverly Potter

Managing Yourself for Excellence
How to Become a Can-Do Person

Overcoming Job Burnout
How to Renew Enthusiasm for Work

The Worrywart's Companion
Twenty-One Ways to Soothe Yourself & Worry Smart

From Conflict to Cooperation
How to Mediate a Dispute

Finding a Path with a Heart
How to Go from Burnout to Bliss

Preventing Job Burnout
A Workbook

The Way of the Ronin
Riding the Waves of Change at Work

High Performance Goal Setting
Using Intutition to Conceive & Achieve Your Dreams

Beyond Conscious
What Happens After Death

Brain Boosters
Foods & Drugs that Make You Smarter

Youth Extension A to Z

Drug Testing at Work
A Guide for Employers

Passing the Test
An Employee's Guide to Drug Testing

The Healing Magic of Cannabis
It's the High that Heals

Turning Around
Keys to Motivation and Productivity

Table of Contents

We identify the flag with almost everything we hold dear on earth, peace, security, liberty, our family, our friends, our home.... But when we look at our flag and behold it emblazoned with all our rights we must remember that it is equally a symbol of our duties. Every glory that we associate with it is the result of duty done.

—Calvin Collidge

No man is entitled to the blessings of freedom unless he be vigilant in its preservation.

— Douglas MacArthur

In the end, we will remember not the words of our enemies, but the silence of our friends.

—Martin Luther King Jr.

America Needs You

America was founded on principles, a creed—ideas about freedom, human dignity, and social responsibility—making it unique among nations. With the Constitution the Founders established a government based on "federalism" where power is shared between the national and state governments. Our power-sharing form of government is the opposite of "centralized" governments, such as those in England and France, where the national government maintains total power. Checks and balances were built into our governmental structure to guard against the accumulation of too much power in one branch of government. The Founders wanted to make sure that power was kept close to the We the People, preferably at the local level. When the checks and balances are defused so that any one branch, such as the Executive, or one governmental level, such as the federal government, accumulates too much power, tyranny is not far behind.

It is upon We the People to be vigilant.

Under federalism, each State is sovereign with its own constitution, but all provisions of State constitutions must comply with the U.S. Constitution. For example, a State constitution cannot deny accused criminals the right to a trial by jury, as assured by the 6th Amendment to the Constitution. Similarly, national and state governments are granted certain exclusive powers and share other powers.

Exclusive Powers of the National Government	Exclusive Powers of State Governments	Power of the People
Print money (bills and coins)	Establish local governments	Bill of Rights
Declare war	Issue licenses	All power not specifically designated to the national or state government resides in the people
Establish an army and navy	Regulate intra-state (within the state) commerce	
Enter into treaties with foreign governments	Conduct elections	
Regulate commerce between states and international trade	Ratify amendments to the U.S. Constitution	
Establish post offices and issue postage	Provide for public health and safety	
Make laws necessary to enforce the Constitution	Powers neither delegated to the national government or prohibited from the States by the U.S. Constitution	

This balance between the National and State governments ought to be dwelt on with peculiar attention, as it is of the utmost importance. It forms a double security to the people. If one encroaches on their rights they will find a powerful protection in the other. Indeed, they will both be prevented from overpassing their constitutional limits by a certain rivalship, which will ever subsist between them.

--Alexander Hamilton
New York Ratifying Convention, 1788

Unfortunately, many Americans don't understand the Constitution and how it protects us from governmental over-reaching by mandating what the government may *not* do to the people. By contrast, the old Soviet Union Constitution spelled out what the government must do *for* the people. As our Founders well knew, it is upon We the People to be vigilant. Government strives to govern. That's just what it does. Government strives to accumulate more and more power so as to extend its governing reach. Left unchecked, government will grow and grow; as it does liberty declines. Our government has been growing for many decades and that expansion has accelerated to taking over private businesses, such as the auto industry, enacting more and more regulations on free enterprise, and ever more regulations that impose upon our private lives and free choices. In the process our liberty is being threatened.

Government expansion will not stop on its own. We the People must act to preserve our free society. Sadly, many Americans are politically illiterate and don't understand the dangers to our freedom. We are Americans! "It" can 'it happened here! But it can and will happen if We the People do not step up and take back America—because government will always take as much power and control as it is permitted to take.

America's motto is *E pluribus Unum*, which translates "Out of many, one" or "Many uniting into one". As Benjamin Franklin emphasized, "Unite or Die". In recent times, power mongers have used race, language, politics, citizenship, and class to divide Americans into hostile balkanized groups to build their power base—just the opposite of what America is about. America became the greatest, wealthiest nation in history

because people from all over the world came to her shores, worked hard, and assumed American values—many uniting into one. When people resist assimilation and cling to their old culture, they are divided. Divided people tend to stick with their "own kind" and to develop animosities towards those who are "different". George Washington understood this when he said, "United we stand; divided we fall."

Many Americans are politically illiterate, yet their votes count as much as literate votes. Politicians know that an uninformed public is easy to sway and direct their campaigns towards apathetic and ignorant voters who outnumber the informed. So demagogues always win as We the People are effectively deprived of the right to self-government.

The 912 Project is a non-partisan, non-political grassroots movement dedicated to restoring America to its founding principles. The 912 groups educate people in America's founding principles and then encourage them to get involved in local politics and work to keep our representative accountable to us—We the People.

The number 912 has two meanings. First, 912 reminds us of 9-12, the day after the horrific attacks on September 11, 2001. On September 12, 2001 we were not obsessed with Red states, Blue states or political parties. We were Americans! We united and we stood together to protect the greatest nation, our nation—the United States of America. The 9-12 Project is a non-political movement aiming to bring us back to the place we were on September 12 when we were pulling together and proud to be Americans!

Second, 912 reminds us of the 9 principles and 12 values that underscored the founding of our nation and have been the bedrock upon which America has stood for over 200 years.

9 Principles

1. America is good.

2. I believe in God and He is the center of my life.

3. I must always try to be a more honest person than I was yesterday.

4. The family is sacred. My spouse and I are the ultimate authority, not the government.

5. If you break the law you pay the penalty. Justice is blind and no one is above it.

6. I have a right to life, liberty and pursuit of happiness, but there is no guarantee of equal results.

7. I work hard for what I have and I will share it with who I want to. Government cannot force me to be charitable.

8. It is not un-American for me to disagree with authority or to share my personal opinion.

9. The government works for me. I do not answer to them, they answer to me.

12 Values

Honesty	Reverence	Hope
Thrift	Humility	Charity
Sincerity	Moderation	Hard Work
Courage	Personal Responsibility	Gratitude

In the past when liberty was threatened, Patriots put on uniforms and went overseas to fight for our freedom. Today Patriots are fighting for freedom right here in the United States because the threats are coming from within. Our weapons are the truth and knowledge—not guns and bombs. Individuals in many towns across the United States have formed 912 organizations and chapters. The aim of these 912 groups is to get the public active in keeping elected officials accountable to voters and taxpayers—to We the People.

The message of the 912 Project should resonate with all Americans who believe in the concepts of Life, Liberty, and the Pursuit of Happiness, which is the heritage of our great nation. 912 is not about political parties; it is not about being a Republican or a Democrat. The 912 Project is about preserving individual liberty by educating Americans in our founding principles and values. 912 groups operate independently. There is no official "leader" or organizational structure. Everyone is a volunteer.

There is much to do. 912 groups around the nation need help. Come pitch in with other Patriots to help save our Republic—America the Beautiful. If you agree with at least 7 out of the 9 Principles and if you live your life by the 12 Values, you are a 9-12er in your heart. I invite you to get involved in a 912 Project—or gather some like-minded folks and start a 912 Project in your area. America needs you! A Google search will bring up 912 groups across the nation—maybe there's one near you. Please join us!

—Mimi Steel
Organizer San Francisco
Bay Area 912 Project

Mimi with Meco, Toes, and Old Glory

Part One

Shining City

America is a shining city upon a hill whose beacon light guides freedom-loving people everywhere.

—Ronald Reagan

The American Dream

The American Dream was coined in 1931 by James Truslow Adams to describe the belief that all citizens, regardless of rank, can create a better, richer, and happier life. There is a widespread determination by Americans to provide their children with a better upbringing than their parents were able to provide for them. It is a philosophy that with hard work, thrift, and determination, anyone can prosper and achieve success.

The American Dream is an entitlement of certain principles of freedom, not of wealth. The American Dream is the promise of an opportunity to *"pursue"* — to have a real shot at developing your abilities and using them to create a better life — as you define it.

The American Dream, that has lured tens of millions of all nations to our shores in the past century has not been a dream of material plenty, though that has doubtlessly counted heavily. It has been a dream of being able to grow to fullest development as a man and woman, unhampered by the barriers which had slowly been erected in the older civilizations, unrepressed by social orders which had developed for the benefit of classes rather than for the simple human being of any and every class.
— James Truslow Adams
The Epic of America

1

American Exceptionalism

America was founded on principles, a creed, a vision of what's possible, making it unique among nations. Other nations found their identity and cohesion in ethnicity, geography, partisan ideology or cultural tradition. America, by contrast, was founded on ideas about freedom, about human dignity, about social responsibility. In the words of President Abraham Lincoln in his Gettysburg Address, America is a nation "conceived in liberty, and dedicated to the proposition that all men are created equal". In this view, being an American is inextricably connected with loving and defending freedom and equal opportunity.

Because American culture emanates from chosen values it is distinct from other nations. America is a society founded on the almost unique belief that who your ancestors are is far less important than who *you* are. This is a monumentally important belief about the worth of the individual. American Exceptionalism is the claim that America and Americans are unique in the world in many important ways, and provides a beacon for hope and opportunity in the world, which Ronald Reagan described as "the last best hope of man on earth."

> America is unique because it was founded on a creed — a vision of liberty for all.

French political thinker and historian Alexis de Tocquerville coined the phrase "American Exceptionalism" in his 1880s book, *Democracy in America*.

*I sought for the greatness and genius of America in her
commodious harbors and her ample rivers, and it was
not there; in her fertile fields and boundless prairies,
and it was not there; in her rich mines and her vast
world commerce, and it was not there. Not until I
went to the churches of America and heard her pulpits
aflame with righteousness did I understand the secret
of her genius and power. America is great because
she is good and if America ever ceases to be good,
America will cease to be great.*

—Alexis de Tocquerville
Democracy in America

Tocqueville identified five values crucial to America's success as a democratic republic: (1) liberty (2) egalitarianism, (3) individualism, (4) populism and (5) laissez-faire. These concepts constitute what is known as the "American Creed". Tocqueville understood these values as being reflective of the absence of feudal and hierarchical structures such as monarchies and aristocracies.

Over the years American Exceptionalism has become an explanation for why and how American society succeeded. The United States was founded by men of conscience who came to the "new world" in order to practice their religious convictions in peace and freedom. It claims that a deliberate choice of freedom over tyranny is the central reason for why American society has been so successful.

The very definition of the term implies that America is different. American Exceptionalists argue that what makes America different is the system of federalism and checks and balances to prevent any person, faction, region, or government organ from becoming too powerful and the accompanying distrust of concentrated power prevents the United States from suffering a tyranny of the majority.

The United States of America, often described as "a shining city on a hill" and nicknamed the "Land of Opportunity", has had less rigid social classes than other nations, and no system of nobility. You rise or fall on your achievement or your failure. That and economic opportunity, which is a result of the American individualist ideal, are the primary reasons why America has been the world's most popular magnet to people from every culture. This is why, historically, America attracts individualists who want to be judged not by their ethnicity, geography, or race, but by who they are. Americans believe that a strong work ethic and personal fortitude are key to success, rather than being born to the right family or making the right friends or living off of the public dole.

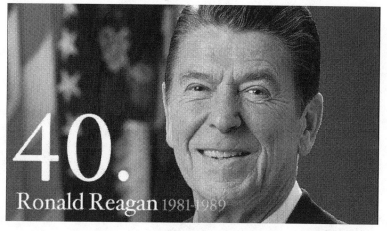

40.
Ronald Reagan 1981-1989

I've spoken of the shining city all my political life.... And how stands the city on this winter night? ... After 200 years, two centuries, she still stands strong and true to the granite ridge, and her glow has held no matter what storm. And she's still a beacon, still a magnet for all who must have freedom, for all the pilgrims from all the lost places who are hurtling through the darkness, toward home.

—Ronald Reagan
Farewell Address

If America is to maintain its exceptionalism—its great experiment in liberty—then there must be an informed patriotism.

2

Informed Citizenry Essential

The purpose of voting, in our country, is to select men and women with the competence and integrity to operate the mechanics of government fixed by our Constitution. These choices must be made on an intelligent, knowledgeable and reasoned basis. As Jefferson said, "an informed citizenry is the bulwark of a democracy".

It is worrisome that the majority of Americans are politically illiterate. The sad thing is, the politically illiterate person's vote counts just as much as the literate vote. Politicians know that an uninformed public is a docile public, easy to sway. They are happy to keep Americans ignorant.

A nation of well-informed men who have been taught to know and prize the rights which God has given them cannot be enslaved. It is in the region of ignorance that tyranny begins.

—Benjamin Franklin

"Any society that would give up a little liberty to gain a little security will deserve neither and lose both."

-Benjamin Franklin

The electoral process has become corrupt. It is not just dead people voting and rigged voting machines. Candidates routinely lie about themselves and their agenda. They base campaign positions on polling data, rather than beliefs and convictions. The media coverage is biased and deceptive.

Campaigns are directed at apathetic and ignorant voters who so outnumber the interested and informed voters that the demagogues always win. The loser is the American people. We are effectively being deprived of our right to self-government.

Big-money contributors buy the ears of the politicians, and the ignorant army of uninformed voters overwhelms those Americans, either liberal or conservative, who have gone to the trouble of educating themselves about the candidates and the issues.

These days politicians sound like social workers. If they are incumbents and feel called upon to defend their records, they talk about what they've done for the people. In the case of federal legislators, what they've done is almost always a list of things that the Constitution forbids them to legislate on. They neglect to say that everything they do is paid for by the American people.

We elect politicians to represent us, so that we do not have to vote on every single issue, which would be impractical. We expect our representatives to be educated about the issues important to us, but how can we reasonably make the decision among candidates and their grasp on issues, if we, ourselves, do not know about the candidates or understand the issues? If we are not educated on the issues, then we cannot make informed decisions regarding the candidates and their stands on those issues.

America will never be destroyed from the outside. If we falter and lose our freedoms, it will be because we destroyed ourselves ... I am a firm believer in the people. If given the truth, they can be depended upon to meet any national crises. The great point is to bring them the real facts.

—Abraham Lincoln

With the advent of the Obama Administration, which controlled both Houses, our representatives—those people we
elected to speak for us—began ramming through 2000 plus
page bills that they had not even read—bills that fundamentally transformed America. Amazingly James Madison, one of
America's Founders, anticipated this deplorable and dangerous
eventuality.

> *It will be of little avail to the people that the laws are
> made by men of their own choice, if the laws be so vo-
> luminous that they cannot be read, or so incoherent that
> they cannot be understood; if they be repealed or revised
> before they are promulgated, or undergo such incessant
> changes that no man who knows what the law is today
> can guess what is will be tomorrow.*

—James Madison
Federalist No. 62

On the eve of passage of Obamacare, which made radical
changes to Americans' health care delivery, then Speaker of
the House, Nancy Pelosi said, "We've got to pass this bill so
that we can find out what is in it." Representatives such as
this beg credibility. These people are not working for We the
People and this is not responsible legislating. Passing laws
without reading them is hardly responsible governing.

If America is to survive as a Shining City on the Hill, as
humanities last great hope for freedom, then we Americans
must become educated in the workings of our amazing system. We must become Patriots and step up to the plate and be
counted. We must take back America.

The Patriots Handbook is offered towards this effort. Read
and then pass it on—one small step for America.

3

We Have Rights

The Preamble to the Declaration of Independence is the foundation of our great nation—the bedrock upon which our liberty and free society have been erected.

We hold these truths to be self-evident, that all men are created equal, that they are endowed by their Creator with certain unalienable Rights, that among these are Life, Liberty and the pursuit of Happiness.

By virtue of being alive we each have unalienable rights. Sometimes called natural rights or moral rights, unalienable rights come from nature—our Creator.

Unalienable rights cannot be surrendered, sold, or transferred. They are endowed upon the individual by the Creator and cannot under any circumstances be surrendered or taken. All individual's have unalienable rights.

Inalienable rights can be surrendered, sold, and transferred *if* you consent. Inalienable rights are not inherent in the individual and can be alienated or taken by government. Most state constitutions recognize only inalienable rights.

Governments derive their "just" power from the permission of those being governed for the purpose of protecting their rights.

That to secure these Rights, Governments are instituted among Men, deriving their just Powers from the Consent of the Governed, that whenever any Form of Government becomes destructive of these Ends, it is the Right of the People to alter or abolish it, and to institute a new Government, laying its Foundations on such Principles and organizing its Powers in such Form, as to Them shall seem most likely to effect their Safety and Happiness.

Should the government fail to protect our rights and act without the consent of the governed, then We the People have the right to change the government in a way that will allow for our unalienable rights to be protected. Governments should not. however, be abolished for trivial reasons.

Prudence, indeed, will dictate that Governments long established should not be changed for light and transient causes; and accordingly all experience hath shewn, that mankind are more disposed to suffer, while evils are sufferable, than to right themselves by abolishing the forms to which they are accustomed. But when a long train of abuses and usurpations, pursuing invariably the same Object evinces a design to reduce them under absolute Despotism, it is their right, it is their duty, to throw off such Government, and to provide new Guards for their future security.

Should the government become abusive and tyrannical, then it is not just the right of the people, but our *duty* to overthrown and replace such a government.

The Declaration of Independence holds no legal authority in our country, yet it continues to be cited as the foundation for American equality.

Important Ideas in the Declaration of Independence

1. All people are created equal.

2. All people have natural rights.

3. Government's authority comes from the people.

4. We the People can change our government if it hurts our natural rights.

4

Independence Declared

The colonists had a long list of grievances against the British Crown. They felt oppressed and tyrannized.

Such has been the patient sufferance of these Colonies; and such is now the necessity which constrains them to alter their former Systems of Government. The history of the present King of Great Britain is a history of repeated injuries and usurpations, all having in direct object the establishment of an absolute Tyranny over these States. To prove this, let Facts be submitted to a candid world.

Here followed a list of grievances
and British Crown abuses.

The colonies made petition after petition to the Crown for redress. But all attempts were ignored.

In every stage of these Oppressions We have Petitioned for Redress in the most humble terms: Our repeated Petitions have been answered only by repeated injury. A Prince whose character is thus marked by every act which may define a Tyrant, is unfit to be the ruler of a free people.

The colonist appealed and warned but it fell on deaf ears.

Nor have We been wanting in attentions to our Brittish brethren. We have warned them from time to time of attempts by their legislature to extend an unwarrantable jurisdiction over us. We have reminded them of the cir-

cumstances of our emigration and settlement here. We have appealed to their native justice and magnanimity, and we have conjured them by the ties of our common kindred to disavow these usurpations, which, would inevitably interrupt our connections and correspondence. They too have been deaf to the voice of justice and of consanguinity. We must, therefore, acquiesce in the necessity, which denounces our Separation, and hold them, as we hold the rest of mankind, Enemies in War, in Peace Friends.

Unable to get any redress, the colonies declared their independence.

We, therefore, the Representatives of the united States of America, in General Congress, Assembled, appealing to the Supreme Judge of the world for the rectitude of our intentions, do, in the Name, and by Authority of the good People of these Colonies, solemnly publish and declare, That these United Colonies are, and of Right ought to be Free and Independent States; that they are Absolved from all Allegiance to the British Crown, and that all political connection between them and the State of Great Britain, is and ought to be totally dissolved; and that as Free and Independent States, they have full Power to levy War, conclude Peace, contract Alliances, establish Commerce, and to do all other Acts and Things which Independent States may of right do. And for the support of this Declaration, with a firm reliance on the protection of divine Providence, we mutually pledge to each other our Lives, our Fortunes and our sacred Honor.

America was born!

5

The Constitution

The United States Constitution is the shortest and oldest written constitution still in use by any nation in the world today. The Constitution was adopted on September 17, 1787, by the Constitutional Convention in Philadelphia, Pennsylvania, and ratified by conventions in each State in the name of "The People". The Constitution has been amended twenty-seven times; the first ten Amendments are known as the Bill of Rights.

The Constitution is the foundation and source of the legal authority underlying the existence of the United States of America and the federal government. It is the supreme law of the land. The Constitution provides the framework for the organization of the United States government and for the relationship of the federal government to the States, to citizens, and to all people within the United States.

The Constitution defines the three main branches of government: a legislature, in the form of a bicameral Congress; an executive branch led by the President; and a judicial branch headed by the Supreme Court. The Constitution specifies the powers and duties of each branch. All unenumerated powers are reserved for the States and the people.

Uneunumerated Powers are powers not expressly mentioned in the written text of the Constitution but are inferred from the language, history, and structure of the Constitution.

centuries. By contrast, France has had 10 separate and distinct constitutional orders in the past 200 years..

The Founders who conceived our Constitution created a governmental framework that has served as a model for freedom-loving people all over the world. Principles of American Constitutionalism—separation of powers, the Bill of Rights, a bicameral legislature, and a presidential form of government—have been used by many nations in drafting their constitutions.

Nearly all of the national constitutions now in use around the world bear the marks of the 55 men who met in Philadelphia in the summer of 1787 to create the framework of the United States government. Like the U.S. Constitution, they are written constitutions. They also spell out human and civil rights similar to those contained in our Constitution. A bill of rights is common.

What is remarkable is that the basic framework of American government has remained unchanged even though the United States has been radically transformed over the past two centuries. Its population has soared from 4 million to nearly 300 million. The federal budget has risen from $4 million in 1790 to over $1 trillion today.

The Constitution is a *charter of negative liberties* to keep government in check. The Founders believed that people cannot be trusted with unchecked power because self-interest and lust for power is too much to resist. Governmental authority must be limited to protect the people from government's tendency to over-reach. The Founders looked to history for workable ideas. They rejected a loose confederation because it would inevitably weaken and degenerate into monarchy or tyranny.

Thomas Jefferson 1801-1809

Republicanism

The Constitution contains an unamendable provision—Article IV, Section 4—that guarantees to every state in this Union a republican form of government. In 1787 "republican" referred to a government in which authority resides in the people, where elected representatives are accountable to the people and must govern according to the law.

The only republics in the world in 1787 were a few small city-states in Italy, Switzerland and the Netherlands. In devising the U.S. Constitution, James Madison sought to create a republic that would endure despite its large size. He argued in the *Federalist Papers* that in a large republic, diverse and conflicting interests would balance and neutralize each other.

> *We have staked the whole of all our political institutions upon the capacity of mankind for self-government, upon the capacity of each and all of us to govern ourselves, to control ourselves, to sustain ourselves according to the Ten Commandments of God.*
>
> —James Madison
> *Founding Father*
> *Fourth President*

The genius of the Constitution was that it created a system of government that used checks and balances to control lust for power while safeguarding individual liberty. Authority was divided between the federal and state governments and was further divided among the three branches of the federal government.

Checks and balances control lust for power and safeguard liberty.

The Preamble

The Preamble began with a grand flourish in laying out the Constitution's *raison d'être*. In its words are the hopes and dreams of the Founders. We are familiar with its words, but may not understand their meaning.

We the People of the United States, in Order to form a
more perfect Union, establish Justice, insure domestic
Tranquility, provide for the common defense, promote
the general Welfare, and secure the Blessings of Liber-
ty to ourselves and our Posterity, do ordain and estab-
lish this Constitution for the United States of America.

The Preamble has no force in law; instead, it establishes the
"why" of the Constitution. It reflects the desires of the Founders to ensure that government would be just, and would protect its citizens from internal strife and from attack from the
outside.

We the People of the United States

While elite themselves, the Founders forged a nation made up
of the common man, not elites. They feared revolution if the
common man was ignored. The Preamble puts on paper that
the people were creating the Constitution, not a god or a king

To Form a More Perfect Union

The Founders were striving for something better than the
Articles of Confederation, which had been a grand experiment that had worked well to a degree, but had been showing
problems. The new United States, under this new Constitution,
would be *more* perfect.

Establish Justice

The people in 1787 were concerned about injustice, unfairness
of laws and in trade. They wanted a nation where courts were
established with uniformity and where trade within and outside the borders of the country was fair and unencumbered.

Insure Domestic Tranquility

The keeping of the peace was a concern. It had not been so long since the Revolution. Then the neophyte nation was hit with a revolt of Massachusetts farmers known as Shays' Rebellion. So maintenance of tranquility was a prime concern. The new powers given the federal government were designed to prevent such rebellions in the future.

Provide for the Common Defense

With a wary eye on Europe, the fledgling nation was fearful of an attack that the states were not capable of fending off an attack from land or sea, except by joining together. Possible Indian attacks were worrisome. To survive, the states needed each other.

Promote the General Welfare

Tranquility, justice, and defense promote the general welfare and allow the states and their citizens to benefit from having a central government.

Secure the Blessings of Liberty

The Founders were striving to secure for all Americans the blessings of liberty, which they had fought hard for a decade to achieve. They were idealistic in their goal of creating a nation that would be a kind of paradise for liberty, rather than the tyranny of a monarchy. The Founders envisioned a nation where citizens did not have to fulfill the interests of a monarch.

Do Ordain and Establish this Constitution for the United States of America

The final clause of the Preamble completes the "We, the people" assertion. It affirms what the people are doing in creating the Constitution and gives it a name, while restating that it is for our country.

The mention of "ordained" reaffirms the influence of the divine in its creation. Finally, the word "establish" means that it replaces the previous Articles of Confederation.

6

Bill of Rights

A central goal of the Founders was to provide Congress with as little power as workable. They were concerned that the lack of specificity would lead to power grabs. Within a few years of the ratification of the Constitution, the Bill of Rights, which includes the first ten Amendments, was added to the Constitution.

Amendment 1
Freedom of Religion, Press, Expression

Congress shall make no law respecting an establishment of religion, or prohibiting the free exercise thereof; or abridging the freedom of speech, or of the press; or the right of the people peaceably to assemble, and to petition the Government for a redress of grievances.

Freedom of Religion

Many consider the 1st Amendment to be the most important Amendment. It contains two clauses about the Freedom of Religion. The first part is known as the Establishment Clause, and the second as the Free Exercise Clause.

The Establishment Clause prohibits the government from passing laws that will establish an official religion or preferring one religion over another. The Courts have interpreted the establishment clause as requiring the separation of church and state.

The Free Exercise Clause prohibits the government from interfering with practice of one's religion. Religious freedom is an absolute right, and includes the right to practice any religion one chooses, or no religion at all, and to do so without government interference. Religious actions and rituals, however, can be limited by civil and federal laws.

The 1st Amendment provides less than full protection to commercial speech, defamation—libel and slander, speech that may be harmful to children, speech broadcast on radio and television, and public employees' speech. Even speech that enjoys the most extensive 1st Amendment protection may be subject to "regulations of the time, place, and manner of expression which are content-neutral, are narrowly tailored to serve a significant government interest, and leave open ample alternative channels of communication."

Free Press

The Founders' conception of freedom of the press has been the subject of intense historical debate, both among scholars and in the pages of judicial opinions. The government may not prevent the publication of a newspaper, even when it reveals information that endangers national security. The government cannot pass a law that requires newspapers to publish information against its will. Except in rare cases neither criminal penalties or civil damages can be imposed by the government on the publication for the nature of its publications. The government cannot impose taxes on the press that it does not levy on other businesses. The government cannot compel journalists to reveal the identities of their sources, with some exceptions. Nor can the government prohibit the press from attending judicial proceedings and thereafter informing the public about them.

This bundle of rights collectively defines the "freedom of the press" guaranteed by the 1st Amendment. What we mean by the freedom of the press is an evolving concept determined by Supreme Court cases.

We have a right to question our government, which exists to protect our unalienable rights.

Freedom of Expression

The Constitution guarantees our freedom to voice our opinions, even if they may be unpopular. Importantly we have a right to question our government. We have a right to dissent—to disagree with the government. We can express our views in words and in art.

A free interchange of ideas is seen as an essential ingredient of democracy and resistance to tyranny, and as an important agent of improvement. We have the liberty to express opinions and ideas without hindrance, and especially without fear of punishment. Freedom of speech as not absolute, however. There are laws regulating incitement, sedition, defamation, slander and libel, blasphemy, the expression of racial hatred, and conspiracy.

Right to Assemble, March, Protest, Petition Government

The Freedom of Assembly Clause—the right to assemble, march, protest, and petition the government—is one of the few Constitutional liberties preceded by a modifier, "peaceably", ensuring that violent uprising and rioting aren't included in the right to gather. "Peaceable" remains the operative word. The 1st Amendment protects peaceful, not violent, assembly, although there must be a "clear and present danger" or an "imminent incitement of lawlessness" in order for government to restrict assembly rights.

The "freedom to peaceably assemble" makes possible the exchange of information and ideas that a democratic society needs to make sound decisions about its own governance. The right to peaceably assemble preserves more than the right to march peacefully. The Court has said you can't deny the right to assemble "without violating those fundamental principles which lie at the base of all civil and political institutions." More profoundly, the Court ruled that "the holding of meetings for peaceable political action cannot be proscribed".

Importance of the 1st Amendment

According to the ACLU, freedom of expression, which encompasses speech, the press, assembly and petition are essential to a free society for four reasons. First, and most importantly, freedom of expression is the foundation of self-fulfillment. Self-expression enables individual to realize their full potential.

Second, freedom of expression is essential to advancement of knowledge. John Stuart Mill, 19th century civil libertarian, said that enlightened judgment is possible only when all facts and ideas are considered, and tested against the conclusions of opposing views. All points of view should be represented in the "marketplace of ideas" so that society can benefit from debate about their worth.

Third, freedom of expression is essential to self-government. To be truly sovereign and masters of our fate and of our elected government, we must be well-informed. To be well-informed we must have access to all information, ideas and points of view.

An informed and enlightened citizenry is a precondition for a free society.

Fourth, freedom of expression helps to keep government corruption and excess in check. The more powerful the government, the more it tends to use its authority to suppress unpopular minorities, criticism and dissent.

Amendment 2
Right to Bear Arms

A well regulated Militia, being necessary to the security of a free State, the right of the people to keep and bear Arms, shall not be infringed.

The meaning of the 2nd Amendment depends upon who you talk to. The National Rifle Association, for example, insists that the Amendment guarantees the right of individuals to possess and carry a wide variety of firearms. Advocates of gun control, on the other hand, contend that the Amendment was only meant to guarantee to States the right to operate militias.

There is on-going debate over the 2nd Amendment. If it does create a right of individuals to own firearms, is the right enforceable against state regulation as well as against federal regulation?

In 2008, the U. S. Supreme Court, in *District of Columbia v. Heller*, struck down a Washington, D.C. ban on individuals having handguns in private homes. Writing for a 5 to 4 majority, Justice Scalia found the right to bear arms to be an individual right consistent with the overriding purpose of the 2nd Amendment, to maintain strong State militias. Scalia wrote that it was essential that the operative clause be consistent with the prefatory clause, but that the prefatory clause did not limit the operative clause.

While the Court found the D. C. law violated the 2nd Amendment's command, it refused to announce a standard of review to apply in future challenges to gun regulations. The Court did say that its decision should not "cast doubt" on laws restricting gun ownership of felons or the mentally ill, and that bans on especially dangerous or unusual weapons would most likely also be upheld. In the 2008 presidential campaign, both major candidates said that they approved of the Court's decision.

Amendment 3
Quartering of Soldiers

No Soldier shall, in time of peace be quartered in any house, without the consent of the Owner, nor in time of war, but in a manner to be prescribed by law.

The first Quartering Act enacted in 1765 required that British soldiers be housed in American barracks and public inns first, but if there was not enough room in these, that other buildings belonging to the citizenry such as stables, alehouses, barns and uninhabited buildings should be used. The Quartering Act required that the citizens who owned the properties must pay for the food for these troops and also stated that the citizens would not receive any compensation for the use of their property.

As a result of this experience with having their private property used by the government without their permission, early Americans wanted a guarantee that they would be protected from this abuse in the future.

The 3rd Amendment is rarely cited in legal cases. The reason it has been cited so few times is that there have been so few wars fought on American territory, especially since the Civil War. Additionally, the US military has sufficient bases to house its soldiers.

Amendment 4
Search and Seizure

> *The right of the people to be secure in their persons, houses, papers, and effects, against unreasonable searches and seizures, shall not be violated, and no Warrants shall issue, but upon probable cause, supported by Oath or affirmation, and particularly describing the place to be searched, and the persons or things to be seized.*

Americans have a long tradition of opposing searches of innocent people which began in Colonial America, when King George's forces searched people indiscriminately in order to uncover a few who were committing offenses against the Crown. These general searches were deeply resented. After the Revolution, the experience of the unfairness of the indiscriminate searches fresh in the new American psyche, the 4th Amendment was passed. It states that authorities cannot search everyone, innocent and guilty alike, to find the few who are guilty—commonly called "going on a fishing trip". There

must be "reasonable suspicion" of particular people before
subjecting them to intrusive or degrading searches.

Privacy

Privacy is one of our fundamental rights granted by the 4th
Amendment. Stated in legal terms, we have a "reasonable
expectation of privacy" in many areas of our lives, such as in
our personal homes, when using bathroom facilities in public
buildings, when talking on the phone, and so forth.

Federal and State constitutions protect all citizens against
unreasonable government searches and seizures of person and
property. Federal protection applies to actions by government
officials, not behavior of private individuals, organizations, or
businesses. Constitutional protections don't apply to privately
held companies.

The right to privacy is not absolute, however, it must be
offset against other compelling interests. An infringement of a
Constitutional privacy right must be justified by a "compelling
public safety interest". Justification for the privacy intrusion
must be substantial to meet the compelling interest test. The
right to pursue and obtain safety, to preserve and protect property, and to pursue and obtain privacy are all protected by the
Constitution. The police conducting a sobriety test at a check-
point is a search. But it is considered to be reasonable because
the public safety considerations outweigh the privacy rights of
the vehicle driver.

Privacy is constantly evolving and being defined by the
Courts. The internet and terrorist activity further challenges
and defines our rights to privacy. In 2010 the government
declared that people do not have "privacy of place", meaning
where we are physically, which can be tracked through cell
phones, is not private.

Arguments surrounding the right to privacy hinge on the
interpretation and application of several key terms and ideas.

These include "search", "seizure", "reasonableness" (as in reasonable expectation of privacy and reasonable suspicion), "probable cause", "compelling interest", and "particularized suspicion".

Searches Must Be Reasonable

There must be a strong indication of particular wrong doing. In general, the rules for violating privacy have to do with "reasonable suspicion" and "probable cause". Reasonableness depends on two factors: the degree of intrusiveness of the search and seizure, and the public interests at stake. A search in the service of public safety, as in the case of an airline pilot, is considered more reasonable than a random search of passengers' luggage on a passenger train, for example.

Reasonable suspicion may be based upon indications that you have committed a crime. Drug Testing, fingerprinting, drawing blood, investigatory stops of motorists at sobriety checkpoints are all examples of various kinds of "searches" that are generally considered lawful invasions of privacy because of public safety concerns, which constitutes compelling interest.

Amendment 5

Trial and Punishment,
Compensation for Takings

No person shall be held to answer for a capital, or otherwise infamous crime, unless on a presentment or indictment of a Grand Jury, except in cases arising in the land or naval forces, or in the Militia, when in actual service in time of War or public danger; nor shall any person be subject for the same offense to be twice put in jeopardy of life or limb; nor shall be compelled in any criminal case to be a witness against himself, nor be deprived of life, liberty, or property, without due process of law; nor shall private property be taken for public use, without just compensation.

Equal Justice Under the Law

"[N]o state shall ... deny to any person within its jurisdiction the equal protection of the laws". The Equal Protection Clause can be seen as an attempt to secure the promise of the United States' professed commitment to the proposition that "all men are created equal" by empowering the judiciary to enforce that principle against the States. However, it grants equal protection, not equal rights.

Equal justice under the law is the bedrock of America's freedom. The due process clause means that the government must respect *all* of the legal rights that are owed to a person according to the law. In America, due process protects individuals from the State and the government is subservient to the law of the land.

The Due Process Clause gives a remedial option, if our Constitutional rights have been violated, as well as imposing unenumerated restrictions on legal procedures.

Self-Incrimination

The 5th Amendment can be asserted in any proceeding, civil or criminal, administrative or judicial, investigatory or adjudicatory. It protects against any disclosures, which the witness reasonably believes could be used in a criminal prosecution or could lead to other evidence that might be so used. For example, a reasonable belief that information concerning income or assets might be used to establish criminal failure to file a tax return can support a claim of 5th Amendment privilege.

Double Jeopardy

The 5th Amendment mandates that should defendants be acquitted on a charge, they may not be tried again for the same offense at the same jurisdictional level. Defendants may be tried again, however, if the previous trial ended in a mistrial or hung jury; if there is evidence of fraud in the previous trial; or if the charges are not precisely the same.

The Miranda Rule

Suspects may not know their rights granted by the 5th Amendment and may make incriminating statements to police officers that they wouldn't have said had they known the law. Suspects' ignorance regarding their civil rights can be used to build a defense case. In *Miranda v. Arizona* (1966), the Supreme Court case created the statement officers are required to issue upon arrest—beginning with the words "You have the right to remain silent...". We've heard it countless times in TV crime shows. Should the officer fail to read the Miranda Rights, a confession and other statements can be "thrown out of Court".

Property Rights and the Takings Clause

The 5th Amendment also protects basic property rights. Under this clause, referred to as the Takings Clause, the government can't simply claim eminent domain and take a citizen's property. The Supreme Court case, *Kelo v. New London* (2005) weakened the protections of the takings clause considerably.

Amendment 6
Right to Speedy Trial,
Confrontation of Witnesses

In all criminal prosecutions, the accused shall enjoy the right to a speedy and public trial, by an impartial jury of the State and district wherein the crime shall have been committed, which district shall have been previously ascertained by law, and to be informed of the nature and cause of the accusation; to be confronted with the witnesses against him; to have compulsory process for obtaining witnesses in his favor, and to have the Assistance of Counsel for his defence.

Adequate Notice

The 6th Amendment guarantees a criminal defendant the fundamental right to be clearly informed of the nature and course of the charges in order to permit adequate preparation of a defense.

Speedy Trial

The speedy trial clause is intended to prevent long-term incarceration and detention without trial, which amounts to a prison sentence without a guilty verdict.

Public Trial

The right to a public trial is to ensure that the proceedings are not conducted in an underhanded way. One question under debate in the Court system is whether *televised* trials protect this right, or exploit it?

Impartial Jury

Jurors must be impartial. They cannot be prejudiced against the accused or the crime of which they have been accused. Additionally, the trial must be held in the area where the crime was committed.

Right to Confront Accuser

The accused has the right to know who is saying what about them and to interrogate the accuser. The accused has the right to ask the Court to issue a summons—or subpoena—to force witnesses and experts to appear and testify at their trial.

Right to Counsel

The accused has the right to an attorney. If they cannot afford an attorney, one is assigned by the Court without a fee. Whenever someone is arrested they are read their Miranda rights. These rights include the right to be silent, and the right to an attorney.

Amendment 7
Trial by Jury in Civil Cases

In Suits at common law, where the value in controversy shall exceed twenty dollars, the right of trial by jury shall be preserved, and no fact tried by a jury, shall be otherwise re-examined in any Court of the United States, than according to the rules of the common law.

The 7th Amendment to the U.S. Constitution guarantees the right to a jury trial in most civil suits that are heard in Federal Court. However, a lawsuit must satisfy four threshold requirements before the 7th Amendment right to a jury trial attaches. The 7th Amendment requires jury trials in civil lawsuits where ordinary damages are sought. A lawsuit must assert a claim for more than $20 and be brought in Federal Court before a litigant may invoke the 7th Amendment right to a jury trial. Finally, a lawsuit must assert a claim that is essentially legal in nature before the 7th Amendment applies.

Together with the Due Process Clause of the 5th Amendment, the 7th Amendment guarantees civil litigants the right to an impartial jury. The presence of even one partial, biased, or prejudiced juror creates a presumption that the 7th Amendment has been violated.

The Courts of Equity

The references to "common law" rely on a distinction found in the British Court system between suits of common law, which were resolved by juries with damages awarded, and suits filed in the court of equity, which were resolved by judges with action taken to correct an unjust situation.

Amendment 8
Cruel and Unusual Punishment

Excessive bail shall not be required, nor excessive fines imposed, nor cruel and unusual punishments inflicted.

Bail is Crucial

Defendants are released on bail so that they may more easily prepare their defense. When denied bail they are effectively punished with imprisonment without the benefit of a trial. On the other hand, if the defendant is charged with a serious offense and poses a flight risk and/or great potential danger to the community, then bail may be denied. Thus decisions regarding bail must have serious consideration.

Cruel and Unusual

The 8th Amendment is more clearly affected by societal change than any other Amendment in the Constitution, because the very nature of the phrase "cruel and unusual" appeals to evolving societal standards. The Crimes Act of 1790 mandated the death penalty for treason, along with mutilation of the corpse. By contemporary standards, corpse mutilation would certainly be regarded as cruel and unusual. Floggings were also common at the time of the Bill of Rights, but today floggings would be regarded as cruel and unusual.

Torture of American citizens is prohibited. The 8th Amendment refers to *de facto* punishments—whether they are officially handed down as punishments or not. The Supreme Court found in *Furman v. Georgia* (1972) that the death penalty, when applied capriciously and on a racially discriminatory basis, violates the 8th Amendment. The death penalty was reinstated in 1976 after serious revisions were made.

While the death penalty is legal, crucifixion and death by stoning are unconstitutional. The Courts have ruled that use of the gas chamber is unconstitutional. Hanging and firing squads are constitutional but rarely used.

Amendment 9
Construction of Constitution

The enumeration in the Constitution, of certain rights, shall not be construed to deny or disparage others retained by the people.

Of all the Amendments in the Bill of Rights, none is harder to interpret than the 9th Amendment. At the time it was proposed, there was no mechanism by which the Bill of Rights could be enforced. The Supreme Court had not yet established the power to strike down unconstitutional legislation. The 9th Amendment was added to address the concern that by specifying some rights that the government was not free to violate, there would be the implication that the government was free to violate any rights not specifically protected in the Constitution.

Amendment 10
Powers of the States and People

The powers not delegated to the United States by the Constitution, nor prohibited by it to the States, are reserved to the States respectively, or to the people.

Originally the Bill of Rights did not apply to the States; it applied only to federal law. States had their own constitutions and their own bills of rights. Some states also had slavery, which was protected under the 10th Amendment. The American Civil War made it clear that this wasn't a workable system, so the 14th Amendment extended the Bill of Rights and made it applicable to both State and federal law.

A major 10th Amendment battle took place as the result of 1960s civil rights legislation, which attempted to enforce the 14th Amendment against Southern states that continued to impose second-class citizenship on black residents. Subsequently, most references to "State's rights" in the common political vernacular are actually veiled references to segregation—unfortunate, given that the question of federal v. State's rights is a legitimate issue that the Supreme Court has been attempting to resolve for two centuries.

Essentially the 10th Amendment says that the people are the boss. It makes explicit the idea that the federal government is limited only to the powers it is explicitly granted. Powers not specifically given to the government in the Constitution are given to the States, effectively limiting governmental power.

A free society is a tolerant society. Unlike the cookie-cutter world of the state, where one education system is made to fit all, where one medication must apply to all, where one lifestyle is forced on all.

In a free society, there's room for cranks, misfits, odd-balls, outcasts. They're free to pursue their happiness in their own way.

—Sharon Harris
Advocates for Self-Government

7

Amending the Constitution

A mendments to the Constitution come about for a reason—it might be to overrule a Supreme Court decision, to
force a societal change, to revise the details of the Constitution.
The Founders knew the future holds unforeseen circumstances
so they designed a process to accommodate future conditions
through the Amendment process. Article V outlines how the
Constitution can be amended.

Article V

*The Congress, whenever two thirds of both Houses shall
deem it necessary, shall propose Amendments to this
Constitution, or, on the Application of the Legislatures
of two thirds of the several States, shall call a Convention for proposing Amendments, which, in either Case,
shall be valid to all Intents and Purposes, as Part of this
Constitution, when ratified by the Legislatures of three
fourths of the several States, or by Conventions in three
fourths thereof, as the one or the other Mode of Ratification may be proposed by the Congress; Provided that no
Amendment which may be made prior to the Year One
thousand eight hundred and eight shall in any Manner
affect the first and fourth Clauses in the Ninth Section of
the first Article; and that no State, without its Consent,
shall be deprived of its equal Suffrage in the Senate.*

Amending the Constitution involves two essential steps: Proposal and Ratification.

Proposing an Amendment

A power vested in the Congress is the right to propose Amendments to the Constitution, whenever two-thirds of both Houses shall deem it necessary. Should two-thirds of the State legislatures demand changes in the Constitution, it is the duty of Congress to call a Constitutional Convention. Proposed Amendments shall be valid as part of the Constitution when ratified by the State legislatures or by conventions of three-fourths of the States, as one or the other mode of ratification may be proposed by Congress.

The President pays no role in the formal Amendment process. He has no veto power over an Amendment proposal or ratification.

Ratifying an Amendment

Amendments must be ratified by the States, regardless of how they were proposed. Three-fourths of the State legislatures must approve of the Amendment proposed by Congress, or three-fourths of the States must approve the Amendment via ratifying conventions. The Supreme Court has held that ratification must happen within "some reasonable time after the proposal." Congress has set a term of seven years for ratification with the 18th Amendment.

The Constitution Offers
Four Paths to Amend the Constitution

• Proposal by convention of states, ratification by state conventions (never used)

• Proposal by convention of states, ratification by state legislatures (never used)

• Proposal by Congress, ratification by state conventions (used once)

• Proposal by Congress, ratification by state legislatures (used all other times)

Informal Amendment

The meaning of the Constitution—the way it is interpreted—evolves over time. Constitution interpretation evolves in two ways. First, circumstances change. As an example, the political process has evolved. Political parties with their primaries and conventions are not mentioned in the Constitution, but have become fundamental to the American political system.

The primary way the meaning of the Constitution changes is through the judiciary, which is the ultimate arbiter of how the Constitution is interpreted and wields more power than the Constitution mandated. The Supreme Court is to use the Constitution as a measure of lawfulness. Increasingly, however, the Justices have looked to case law in judicating. But case law is a step removed from the Constitution. This is a back door to the "living Constitution" sought by those who wish to enact unconstitutional impositions upon the People. With the Obama Administration came the introduction of global law as a measure of lawfulness. This is why many believe appointing judges to the Supreme Court is the President's most powerful—and important—act.

Amendments to the Constitution

Amendment 11
Lawsuits Against States

The 11th Amendment clarifies the original jurisdiction of the Supreme Court concerning a suit brought against a state by a citizen of another state. February 7, 1795.

Amendment 12
Presidential Elections

Redefines how the President and Vice-President are chosen by the Electoral College from being first and second highest vote-getters to the positions being cooperative and mandates that the Vice-President must be eligible to become President. June 15, 1804. Superseded by Section 3 of the 20th Amendment.

Amendment 13
Abolition of Slavery

Abolished slavery. December 6, 1865.

Amendment 14
Civil Rights

Removed the three-fifths counting of slaves in the census and ensured that all citizens enjoy rights on both the federal and state levels. The United States would not pay the debts of rebellious states and included measures designed to ensure the loyalty of legislators who participated in the Confederation. July 9, 1868.

Amendment 15
Black Suffrage

Race cannot be used as criteria for voting. February 3, 1870

Amendment 16
Income Taxes

Authorizes the United States to collect income tax without regard to the population of the states. February 3, 1913.

Amendment 17
Senatorial Elections

Shifted election of Senators from the state legislatures to a vote by the people of the states. April 8, 1913.

Amendment 18
Prohibition of Liquor

Prohibited the sale, manufacture, and transport of alcohol for the purposes of alcoholic beverages. January 16, 1919.

Amendment 19
Women's Suffrage

Gender cannot be used as criteria for voting. August 18, 1920.

Amendment 20
Terms of Office

Established end dates for the terms of the Congress and the President. Clarifies the process for transfer of power in the case of the death of the President. January 23, 1933.

Amendment 21
Repeal of Prohibition

Repealed the 18th Amendment. December 5, 1933.

Amendment 22
Term Limits for the Presidency

Set a limit on the number of times a President can be elected to two four-year terms — when Vice-President assumes the Presidency after the death or removal of the President, establishing the maximum term of any President to 10 years. February 27, 1951.

Amendment 23
Washington, DC Suffrage

Grants the District of Columbia (Washington D.C.) the right to three electors in Presidential elections. March 29, 1961.

Amendment 24
Abolition of Poll Taxes

Prohibit any tax being charged to vote for any federal office. January 23, 1964.

Amendment 25
Presidential Succession

Clarifies even the line of succession to the Presidency, and establishes rules for a President who becomes unable to perform his duties while in office. February 10, 1967.

Amendment 26
18-Year-Old Suffrage

Any citizen 18 years old or over has a right to vote. June 30, 1971.

Amendment 27
Congressional Pay Raises

Any law that increased the pay of legislators may not take effect until after an election. May 7, 1992.

Part Two

A Republic

*"Well, Doctor, what have we got—
a Republic or a Monarchy?"*

"A Republic, if you can keep it."

—Ben Franklin

To Be Governed

To be governed is to be watched, inspected, spied upon, directed, law-ridden, regulated, penned up, indoctrinated, preached at, checked, appraised, seized, censured, commanded, by beings who have neither title, nor knowledge, nor virtue.

To be governed is to have every operation, every transaction, every movement noted, registered, counted, rated, stamped, measured, numbered, assessed, licensed, refused, authorized, endorsed, admonished, prevented, reformed, redressed, corrected.

—Pierre-Joseph Proudhon
French political theorist, 1849

Government is Force

Love your country; fear your government.
Only the government can take your property;
Only the government can take your freedom;
Only the government can take your life.

8

Forms of Government

There's a lot of confusion about the political continuum. We usually think of communism as being on the far left, with fascism or dictators being on the far right, and political moderates or centrists being in the middle.

A more accurate model is one with zero government power on the far right continuing to government with total power on the far left. At the extreme right there is no government—anarchy; at the extreme left we find totalitarianism or total government—communism, socialism, Nazism, fascism, dictators, monarchs. In the middle of the political continuum is government limited to protecting the rights of the people. In designing our government the Founders placed us near the right, with a small government, limited by the terms of the Constitution.

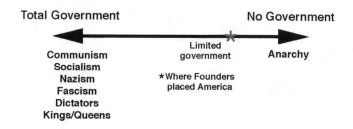

Monarchy/Dictatorship
Rule by One

In a monarchy, the head of state is usually the descendant of a specific noble family that earned the allegiance of other noble families and established a dynasty. The rise of the middle class shifted power from an absolute monarchy (total power within the king or queen) towards the constitutional monarchies found in England and other countries today, which serve as living symbols of the past heritage.

Dictators generally arise from the lower classes or the military and assume power outside of normal political processes. Sometimes, dictators become kings to establish legitimacy, with the hope of establishing a new dynasty, as with Napoleon. While dictators may use legislative bodies to rubber stamp their initiatives, all power is concentrated in the dictator. Hitler did not disband the Reichstag when he assumed power, for example. Stalin was "elected" to his post—with no opposition, of course.

Theocracy
Rule by God

"Theocracy" means a rule by God in Greek. In a theocracy, the rule of law merges with the canon of an organized religion. Earthly human matters are governed by divine guidance bestowed on religious institutional representatives such as "The Church", Sharia, or Islamic law. Other examples are Geneva under Calvin's rule in the 16th century and the Pilgrims in control of the Massachusetts Colony in the 17th century.

Oligarchy
Rule by a Few

Oligarchy is derived from the Greek word for "few" and "rule". Oligocracy is a government controlled by powerful elites whose power is derived from wealth, royalty, family, religious hegemony, intellectual achievement, military strength, ruthlessness, or political influence.

Democracy
Rule by the Majority

In Greek, democracy means "popular government". A direct democracy is a system of government in which governing is carried out by the people governed, whereas in representative democracy the power to govern is granted by the people. That is, the people elect officials to represent their interests.

In direct democracies, the majority's power is absolute and unlimited; its decisions are unappealable under the legal system established to give effect to this form of government, which opens the door to tyranny by the majority. This was what the Founders were concerned about when speaking of the "excesses of democracy" and abuses of the unalienable rights of the individual by the majority.

In Rousseau's view, because a democratic government embodies the general will of the people, it will always be right. Thus government should have absolute, centralized power over a militarized and unified egalitarian nation-state. Attitude toward law is that the will of the majority shall regulate — regardless if it is driven by deliberation or passion, prejudice, and impulse.

A democracy must be carefully legislated with balances to avoid an uneven distribution of political power, such as separation of powers, to prevent one branch of the system of rule from accumulating too much power. "Majority rule" is often described as a characteristic feature of democracy, but the danger is that dissenting individuals are oppressed by the "tyranny of the majority".

Anarchy
Rule by No One

Anarchy is derived from the Greek for "without ruler" and refers to a state of lawlessness and political disorder result-

ing from an absence of government so there is no rulership or
enforced authority and each individual has absolute liberty.
Anarchy is oppressive. There is little freedom in having to be
constantly armed to protect your life, liberty and property.

Anarchy creates a vacuum that is quickly filled by the
strongest factions with the most weapons or other power and
evolves into an oligarchy.

Republic
Rule by Law

A Republic is a limited representative government, created by
a written Constitution—adopted by the electorate. Its powers are divided between three separate branches—Executive,
Legislative and Judicial. It is a government system, designed
to control the majority strictly, with the purpose of protecting
the individual's God-given, unalienable rights. A Republic
protects of the rights of the minority, of all minorities, and the
liberties of people in general.

Totalitarianism
Rule by Force

Totalitarianism is a political system in which the government's
authority is unlimited and regulates every aspect of public and
private life. Totalitarianism means total government rule. Totalitarian governments generally discourage, even persecute,
free will and free expression.

Many of the worst crimes against humanity, such as the
holocaust, have been committed by totalitarian governments.
But no government—anarchy—such as in Somalia where
pirates rule is also oppressive—and certainly not safe. The
Ancient Greeks wisely observed, "Without law there can be no
freedom". The Founding Fathers were suspicious of government, but understood that some government is necessary for a
civilized orderly society.

Socialism

Socialism—workers' state—represents the interests of the working class and often endorse Marxism-Leninism ideology. Socialistic governments take care of workers with social welfare provisions, such as healthcare and unemployment benefits, within a capitalist system.

The statist doctrines of Marx and Keynes, allege that society cannot run itself; instead the general will, the interests of the proletariat, or the economic plans of the people need to be organized and embodied in the nation and its head. This is a view of government that the Founders rightly saw as despotic, and sought to prevent from taking root in America.

Communism

Communism is a social structure in which classes are abolished and property is commonly controlled by the collective. As a social movement, communism aims to overthrow the capitalist order by revolutionary means and to establish a classless society in which all goods will be socially owned.

Communism has ten essential planks:

- Abolition of private property.
- Heavy progressive income tax.
- Abolition of rights of inheritance.
- Confiscation of property rights.
- Government controlled central bank.
- Government ownership of communication and transportation.
- Government ownership of factories and agriculture.
- Government control of labor.
- Corporate farms and regional planning.
- Government control of education.

—The Communist Manifesto

How communism differs from socialism has long been a matter of debate. Communism tends to adhere to the revolutionary notions of Karl Marx, whereas socialism works towards evolutionary change.

Socialism generally refers to an economic system, while communism generally refers to both an economic and a political system. As an economic system, socialism seeks to manage the economy through deliberate and collective social control. Communism, however, seeks to manage both the economy and the society by ensuring that property is owned collectively, and that control over the distribution of property is centralized in order to achieve both classlessness and statelessness. Both socialism and communism seek to prevent what they see as ill effects produced by capitalism.

Both socialism and communism are based on the principle that the goods and services produced in an economy should be owned publicly, and controlled and planned by a centralized organization. Socialism asserts that the distribution should take place according to the amount of individuals' production efforts, while communism asserts that goods and services should be distributed among the populace according to individuals' needs.

Another distinction is that communists assert that both capitalism and private ownership of the means of production must be done away with as soon as possible in order to make sure a classless society—the Communist Ideal—is formed. Socialists, however, see capitalism as a possible part of the Ideal State and believe that socialism can exist in a capitalist society. In fact, one of the ideals of socialism is that everyone within the society benefits from capitalism as much as possible as long as the capitalism is controlled somehow by a centralized planning system.

Fascism

Fascism is a political regime rooted in an ideology that holds the State—or sometimes religion as in some Muslin countries—as supreme over individual rights and is often lead by a cult-like personality. The State is usually totalitarian with the government controlling business and repressing criticism and opposition.

The State controls all aspects of manufacturing, commerce, finance, and agriculture. Planning boards set product lines, production levels, prices, wages, working conditions, and the size of firms.

Where socialism seeks totalitarian control of a society's economic processes through direct State operation of the means of production, fascism seeks that control indirectly, through domination of nominally private owners. Where socialism nationalizes property explicitly, fascism does it by requiring owners to use their property in the "national interest" as conceived by its autocratic authority. Where socialism abolishes all market relations outright, fascism leaves the appearance of market relations while planning all economic activities. Where socialism abolishes money and prices, fascism controls the monetary system and sets all prices and wages politically.

Fascism's approach to politics is both populist—it seeks to activate "the people" as a whole against perceived oppressors or enemies, and elitist—it treats the people's will as embodied in a select group or a supreme leader, from whom authority proceeds downward.

Capitalism

Capitalism is an economic system that thrives under limited government. Under capitalism, the means of production are privately owned. Supply, demand, price, distribution, and investments are determined mainly by private decisions and market forces. Profit—and loss—is distributed to the business owners who took the risks.

In a capitalist system, the government does not prohibit private property or determine where individuals work. Businesses determine what wages they pay and what prices they charge for their products, not the government—although many countries have minimum wage laws and minimum safety standards.

Many economists argue that the economic freedom of capitalism is a requisite of political freedom. Milton Friedman maintains that centralized control of economic activity is always accompanied by political repression. In his view, transactions in a market economy are voluntary, and the wide diversity that voluntary activity permits is a fundamental threat to repressive political leaders and greatly diminish power to coerce. Economists, Friedrich Hayek and John Maynard Keynes argue that capitalism is vital for freedom to survive and thrive.

Government has no power and no resources that it doesn't first take from the people. Unlike private enterprise, it cannot produce anything. Whatever it has, it must extract from private enterprise.

—Llewellyn H. Rockwell, Jr.
Ludwug von Mises Institute

9

Democracy or Republic

A merica is a republic, not a pure democracy. Understanding the difference between the two forms of government is essential to comprehension of the fundamentals involved. A democracy is controlled by the majority and lacks any legal safeguards for the rights of the individual, whereas in a republic the power of the majority is limited under a written Constitution to safeguard the rights of the individual and the minority.

What makes America a republic is our tradition of adhering to the Rule of Law—The Constitution. The people have representation through the legislature, but legislature is limited by the rules of the Constitution, which is designed to be very difficult to change through the laborious Amendment process. If we didn't have such a strict Constitution, we'd have a pure democracy—or mob rule.

> *Democracies have ever been spectacles of turbulence and contention; have ever been found incompatible with personal security or the rights of property; and have in general been as short in their lives as they have been violent in their deaths.*
> —James Madison
> *Federalist #10*

Democracy

The chief characteristic and distinguishing feature of a democracy is rule by an omnipotent majority. When more than half the population gets power it becomes a mobocracy. Democracy is government by the masses, which are not restrained. Instead restraint is upon the individual, not the government.

A democracy is nothing more than mob rule where fifty-one percent of the people may take away the rights of the other forty-nine.

—Thomas Jefferson

There is no legal protection for the minority party in a democracy. There are no unalienable rights for the minority unless the majority agrees.

In a democracy, the majority rules either directly or through its elected representatives. The law is whatever the government determines it to be. Rights are seen as privileges granted by government and can be rescinded by government. In our Constitution government is a protector of our unalienable rights—not the grantor.

The will of the majority governs by passion, prejudice, and impulse, without restraint, which leads to demagogism, license, agitation, discontent, and anarchy. Authority in a democracy is derived through mass meetings or other forms of direct expression.

The people vote on everything that has to do with governing in a democracy. Laws and other major decisions require a majority vote of the people to pass. Pure democracies have only been tried on relatively small scale societies and have never really worked because most people don't have the time to study the issues while doing all the other things that they have to do to make a living.

The Founders honored the spirit of the free man and decried the "excesses of democracy". They knew from history that only a republic can provide safeguards for individual liberties, which are inescapably victimized by democracy's system of unlimited government-over-man featuring the majority omnipotent.

Democracy	Republic
Majority rule. No safe guards for minority or individual.	Majority is limited by safe guards for individual and minority.
Rule by omnipotent majority with no protection against the unlimited power of the majority.	Rule by elected representatives to make sure that minority views are considered.
The majority's power is absolute and unlimited; its decisions are unappealable under the legal system established to give effect to this form of government.	Constitutionally limited government of the representative type.
Neither the courts nor any other part of the government can effectively challenge or block actions by the majority in the legislative body, no matter how arbitrary, tyrannous, or totalitarian.	The majority is controlled to protect the rights of the minority

Republic

Many people think democracy and republic are synonyms, which they aren't. The difference between a republic and a democracy is in the source of its official power. A republic is a political unit governed by a charter, whereas a democracy is a government ruled by the majority opinion.

The republic exists to protect the individual's God-given, unalienable rights and the liberties of the people. A republic is a constitutionally limited government of the representative type, created by a written Constitution, adopted by the people and changeable by them only by Amendment, with its powers divided between three separate branches: Executive, Legislative and Judicial. Here the term "the people" means the electorate.

In a republic, authority is derived through the election of public officials by the people to represent them. Justice is administered in accord with fixed principles and established evidence. A republic avoids the dangerous extremes of tyranny and mobocracy and promotes statesmanship, liberty, reason, justice, contentment, and progress.

The people "hire" individuals to make decisions and pass the needed laws. Those who want to govern campaign for the approval of the citizenry and are chosen by way of voting. Freedom is realized by the willingness of the people to live by the dictates of the charter—the Constitution. The republic's charter protects the individual's rights.

A republic bars equally the "snob-rule" of a governing elite and the "mob-rule" of an omnipotent majority—both of which tend to be hostile to individual liberty.

America the Beautiful

O beautiful for spacious skies,
For amber waves of grain,
For purple mountain majesties
Above the fruited plain!
America! America!
God shed his grace on thee
And crown thy good with brotherhood
From sea to shining sea!
                                    —Katharine Lee Bates

10

Separation of Powers

A s delegates to the Constitutional Convention the Founders faced a difficult challenge. Because of the colonies' experience under the British monarchy, they wanted to avoid giving any one person or group absolute control in government. They wanted to ensure a strong, cohesive central government, yet they also wanted to ensure that no individual or small group in the government would become too powerful. Under the Articles of Confederation, the government had lacked centralization, and the Founders didn't want to have that problem again. To solve these problems, they created a government with three separate branches, each with its own distinct powers. This system would establish a strong central government, while insuring a balance of power.

The structure of American government is spelled out in the Constitution. The inspiration for the separation of powers amongst different branches of government can be traced to ancient Greece. The Founders of the Constitution decided to base the American governmental system on this idea of three separate branches: executive, judicial, and legislative. The three branches are distinct and have checks and balances to prevent tyrannous concentration of power in any one branch and to protect the rights and liberties of citizens.

Checks and Balances

The American Constitution includes a system of checks and balances to guarantee that no part of the government becomes too powerful. The legislative branch is in charge of making laws. The President can veto bills approved by Congress and the President nominates individuals to serve in the federal judiciary, or an action by the President unconstitutional; and Congress can impeach the President and federal court justices and judges thus making it harder for the legislative branch to pass the law. The judicial branch can "check" the law if they find it "unconstitutional". While the executive branch appoints judges, the legislative branch must approve them. The legislative branch can remove presidents and judges who are not performing their job properly. In this way, no one branch can gain absolute power or abuse the power they are given.

Executive Branch

When the Founders created the executive branch of government, they gave the President a limited term of office to lead the government. This was different from Europe governments and caused much debate. The Founders were afraid of what too much power in the hands of one person. In the end, with a system of checks and balances included in the Constitution, a single President to manage the executive branch of government was adopted.

1. George Washington 1789-1797

The executive branch of the government is responsible for enforcing the laws of the land. When George Washington was president, people recognized that one person could not carry out the duties of the President without advice and assistance. The Vice President, Cabinet members, and heads of independent agencies assist in this capacity. Unlike the powers of the President, their responsibilities are not defined in the Constitution but each has special powers and functions.

- **President:** Leader of the country and Commander in Chief of the military.

- **Vice President:** President of the Senate and becomes President if the President is unable to serve.

- **Departments:** Department heads advise the President on policy issues and help execute those policies.

- **Independent Agencies:** Help execute policy or provide special services.

Judicial Branch

Article III of the Constitution established the judicial branch of government with the creation of the Supreme Court. This court is the highest court in the country and vested with the judicial powers of the government. There are lower Federal courts but they were not created by the Constitution. Rather, Congress deemed them necessary and established them using power granted from the Constitution.

Courts decide arguments about the meaning of laws, how they are applied, and whether they violate the Constitution. The latter power is known as judicial review and it is this process that the judiciary uses to provide checks and balances on the legislative and executive branches. Judicial review is not an explicit power given to the courts but it is an implied power. In a landmark Supreme Court decision, *Marbury v. Madison* (1803), the courts' power of judicial review was clearly articulated.

Legislative Branch

Article I of the Constitution established the legislative or law-making branch of government with the formation of a bicameral—two-part—Congress. This system provides checks and balances within the legislative branch.

Only after much debate did the Founding Fathers agree on the creation of the House of Representatives and the Senate. A major issue was how representation in the legislative body would be determined. Delegates to the Constitutional Convention from larger and more populated states argued for the Virginia Plan that called for congressional representation based on a state's population. Fearing domination, delegates from smaller states were just as adamant for equal representation and supported the New Jersey Plan. Roger Sherman, a delegate from Connecticut, proposed the bicameral legislature. The Great Compromise, among other provisions, resulted in the creation of two houses, with representation based on population in one and with equal representation in the other.

Members of Congress are now elected by a direct vote of the people of the state they represent. Senators have not always been selected this way. Prior to 1913 and ratification of the 17th Amendment to the Constitution, Senators were chosen by their state legislatures because the Senate was viewed as representative of state governments, not of the people. It was the responsibility of Senators to ensure that their state was treated equally in legislation.

Agencies that provide support services for the Congress are also part of the legislative branch. These include the Government Printing Office (GPO), the Library of Congress (LC), the Congressional Budget Office (CBO), the Government Accountability Office (GAO), and the Architect of the Capitol.

11

The Executive Branch

The Executive Branch of government is headed by the President of the United States, who also acts as the head of state in diplomatic relations and as Commander-in-Chief of all U.S. branches of the armed forces. The President is responsible for implementing and enforcing the laws written by Congress and, to that end, appoints the heads of the federal agencies, including the Cabinet. The Vice President is also part of the Executive Branch, and must remain ready to assume the presidency should the need arise. While the President has significant power, his power is limited by the Constitution.

Article II, section 1, of the Constitution provides that *"[t]he executive Power shall be vested in a President of the United States of America. He shall hold his Office during the Term of four Years, . . . together with the Vice President, chosen for the same Term . . . ."*

Powers assigned to the President:

- Commander in Chief of the Armed Forces.

- Make treaties, with two-thirds consent of the Senate.

- Receive ambassadors and other public ministers from foreign countries.

- Appoint ambassadors, Supreme Court justices, federal judges, and any officials as provided for by the Congress, with the approval of the Senate.

- Give an annual State of the Union Address to Congress.

- Recommend legislation to Congress.

- Convene Congress on extraordinary occasions.
- Adjourn Congress, in cases of a disagreement about adjournment.
- "Take care that the laws be faithfully executed".
- Fill in administrative vacancies during Congressional recesses.
- Grant reprieves and pardons for offences against the U.S.

These powers fall into three categories: Head of State, Administrative, and Legislative Powers.

Head of State

As Head of State, the President meets with the leaders of other countries. He has the power to recognize those lands as official countries and to make treaties with them. However, the Senate must approve any treaty before it becomes official. The President also has the power to appoint ambassadors to other countries, with the Senate's approval.

The President is the official head of the U.S. military. As Commander in Chief, he can authorize the use of troops overseas without declaring war. To declare war officially, though, he must get the approval of the Congress.

Administrative Powers

The President's administrative duties include appointing the heads of each executive branch department. Of course, these appointments are subject to the approval of the Senate. The President also has the power to request the written opinion of the head of each executive branch department, regarding any subject relating to their department.

Legislative Powers

Most people view the President as the most powerful and influential person in the United States government. While he does wield a great deal of political might, his effect on the law-making process is limited. Only Congress can write legislation; the President may only recommend legislation. If he does so, then a member of Congress may introduce the bill for consideration.

Whereas only Congress may create legislation, it is difficult for them to pass a bill without the President's approval. When Congress passes a bill, they send it to the White House. The President then has three options: sign the bill into law, veto the bill, or do nothing.

When the President signs a bill into law, it immediately goes into effect. At this point, only the Supreme Court can remove the law from the books by declaring it unconstitutional.

Presidential Veto Power

When the President vetoes a bill, it does not go into effect. The President vetoes a bill by returning it to Congress unsigned. In most cases, he will also send them an explanation of why he rejected the legislation. Congress can override a presidential veto, but to do so, two-thirds of each chamber must vote in favor of the bill. Such an override is rare.

If the President chooses the third option, doing nothing with the bill, one of two things will occur. If Congress is in session ten business days after the President receives the bill, the legislation will become a law without the President's signature. However, if Congress adjourns within ten business days of giving the bill to the President, the bill dies. When the President kills a bill in this fashion, it is known as a pocket veto. In this case, Congress can do nothing to override his decision.

The Presidential veto is an extremely powerful tool. Often, to get Congress to reconsider legislation, the President need only threaten to veto a bill if it passes.

However, this power has its limitations. The President may only veto a bill in its entirety; he does not have the power of a line-item veto, which would allow him to strike individual sections of a bill while still passing it. Because of this limitation, the President must often compromise if Congress passes a bill that he agrees with, but attaches a rider that goes against his policy.

Compromise, in general, is a crucial aspect to a President's success in working with Congress. The President's political party very rarely also controls Congress. Thus most of the time, the President must work with Senators and Representatives who disagree with his agenda. However, if the President refused to pass any legislation that he disagreed with and Congress behaves similarly, the government would come to a halt. Thus, they must work together to keep the government moving.

In addition, the President relies on the support of the American people to accomplish his goals. The public elects the President and the members of Congress. When the public disapproves of the President, Senators and Representatives will distance themselves from the President and his agenda. If they side with an unpopular President, their constituents might not re-elect them. Thus, if the President loses popular support, he will lose support in Congress and will have great difficulty getting his suggested legislation enacted.

Requirements and Term

The President and the Vice-President are the only officials elected by the entire country. There are, however, requirements for holding either of these positions. In order to be elected, one must be at least 35 years old. Also, each candidate must be a natural-born U.S. citizen and have lived in the U.S. for at least 14 years.

When elected, the President serves a term of four years. At most, a President may serve two terms. However, before 1951, the President could serve as many terms as he wanted. Every President followed George Washington's example of stepping down after two terms until Franklin D. Roosevelt broke with tradition, when he ran for office four times. Early in his fourth term, in 1945, Franklin died. Six years later, Congress passed the 22nd Amendment to limit Presidents to two terms.

Impeachment

The President can be removed from office through the process of impeachment. If the House of Representatives feels that the President has committed acts of "Treason, Bribery, or other High Crimes and Misdemeanors" they can impeach him with a majority vote. An impeachment is very similar to a legal indictment. It is not a conviction, however, and not enough to remove the President from office.

The case then goes to the Senate. Overseen by the Chief Justice of the Supreme Court, the Senate reviews the case and votes whether or not to convict the President. If they vote in favor of conviction by a two-thirds margin, then the President is removed from office.

The President's Cabinet

The purpose of the Cabinet is to advise the President on matters relating to the duties of their respective offices. As the President's closest and most trusted advisors, members of the Cabinet meet weekly with the President. The Constitution does not directly mention a "Cabinet," but the Constitutional authority for a Cabinet is found in Article II, Section 2. The Constitution states that the President "may require the opinion, in writing of the principle officer in each of the executive departments, upon any subject relating to the duties of their respective offices." The Constitution does not say which or how many executive departments should be created.

The Cabinet traditionally includes the Vice President and the heads of 15 executive departments-the Secretaries of Agriculture, Commerce, Defense, Education, Energy, Health and Human Services, Homeland Security, Housing and Urban Development, Interior, Labor, State, Transportation, Treasury, and Veterans Affairs, and the Attorney General. Cabinet-level rank has also been given to the Administrator of the Environmental Protection Agency; the Director of the Office of Management and Budget; the Director of the National Drug Control Policy; the Assistant to the President for Homeland Security; and the U.S. Trade Representative.

The fifteen Secretaries from the executive departments are appointed by the President and must be confirmed by a majority vote—51 votes—of the Senate. Cabinet appointments cannot be a member of Congress or hold any other elected office. The appointments are for the duration of the administration, but the President may dismiss any member at any time, without approval of the Senate. Cabinet members are expected to resign when a new President takes office.

Cabinet

When requested by the President, other officials are asked to attend these weekly meetings including, the President's Chief of Staff, the Director of the Central Intelligence Agency, the Chairman of the Council of Economic Advisors, the Counselor to the President, the Director of the Federal Emergency Management Agency, the Administrator of the Small Business Administration, and the U.S. Representative to the United Nations.

Order of Succession

According to the Presidential Succession Act of 1947, if the President of the United States is incapacitated, dies, resigns, is for any reason unable to hold his office, or is removed from office (impeached and convicted), people in the following offices, in this order, will assume the office of the President, provided they are qualified as stated by the Constitution to assume the office of the President, which means they have to be must be at least 35 years old, must be a natural-born U.S. citizen, and have lived in the U.S. for at least 14 years.

Order of Succession

- Vice President
- Speaker of the House
- President Pro Temp of the Senate
- Secretary of State
- Secretary of the Treasury
- Secretary of Defense
- Attorney General
- Secretary of the Interior
- Secretary of Agriculture
- Secretary of Commerce
- Secretary of Labor
- Secretary of Health and Human Services
- Secretary of Housing and Urban Development
- Secretary of Transportation
- Secretary of Energy
- Secretary of Education
- Secretary of Veterans Affairs
- Secretary of Homeland Security

The 25th Amendment of the U.S. Constitution, passed in 1967, provides for procedures to fill vacancies in the Vice Presidency; further clarifies presidential succession rules.

12

The Supreme Court

The Constitution established the Supreme Court as the highest court in the United States. The authority of the Court originates from Article III of the U.S. Constitution and its jurisdiction is set out by statute in Title 28 of the *US Code*.

Article III Section 1

Judicial Powers

> *The judicial Power of the United States shall be vested in one Supreme Court, and in such inferior Courts as the Congress may from time to time ordain and establish. The Judges, both of the supreme and inferior Courts, shall hold their Offices during good Behavior, and shall, at stated Times, receive for their Services a Compensation which shall not be diminished during their Continuance in Office.*

One of the Supreme Court's most important responsibilities is to decide cases that raise questions of constitutional interpretation. The Court decides if a law or government action violates the Constitution. This is known as judicial review and enables the Court to invalidate both federal and state laws when they conflict with the Constitution. Since the Supreme Court stands as the ultimate authority

in constitutional interpretation, its decisions can be changed only by another Supreme Court decision or by a constitutional amendment.

Judicial review puts the Supreme Court in a pivotal role in the American political system, making it the referee in disputes among various branches of the federal, as well as state governments, and as the ultimate authority for many of the most important issues in the country. For example, *Brown* v. *Board of Education* in 1954, the Court banned racial segregation in public schools. The ruling started a long process of desegregating schools and other institutions.

The Supreme Court has the final word on cases heard by federal courts, and it writes procedures that these courts must follow. All federal courts must abide by the Supreme Court's interpretation of federal laws and the Constitution of the United States. The Supreme Court's interpretations of federal law and the Constitution also apply to the state courts, but the Court cannot interpret state law or issues arising under state constitutions, nor does it does not supervise state court operations.

How It Works

Usually cases are first brought in front of a lower—state or federal—court. Each disputing party is made up of a petitioner and a respondent. After the lower court makes a decision, if the losing party does not think that justice was served, the case may be appealed to a higher court. In the state court system, these higher courts are called appellate courts. In the federal court system, the lower courts are called United States District Courts and the higher courts are called United States Courts of Appeals.

Most cases do not start in the Supreme Court. Though not often exercised, original jurisdiction gives the Court the power to sit as a trial court to hear cases affecting ambassadors and other foreign officials, and in cases in which a state is a party. Only disputes between two or more states must be heard initially in the Supreme Court. The 1997-98 dispute between New York and New Jersey over the ownership of Ellis Island is an example of the Supreme Court exercising original jurisdiction.

If the higher court's ruling disagrees with the lower court's ruling, the original decision is overturned. If the higher court's ruling agrees with the lower court's decision, then the losing party may ask that the case be taken to the Supreme Court. But as previously mentioned, only cases involving federal or Constitutional law are brought to the highest court in the land.

Cases Brought Before the Court

Approximately 7,500 cases are sent to the Supreme Court each year. Out of these, fewer than 100 are actually heard by the Supreme Court. When a case goes to the Supreme Court, several things happen. First, the Justices get together to decide if a case is worthy of being brought before the Court. In other words, does the case really involve Constitutional or federal law? Secondly, a Supreme Court ruling can affect the outcome of hundreds or even thousands of cases in lower courts around the country. Therefore, the Court tries to use this enormous power only when a case presents a pressing Constitutional issue.

Once the Justices decide to take a case, the lawyers for each side have one-half hour in which to present their side of the case in what is called "oral argument." The Justices can interrupt to ask questions at any time. It is considered a great honor for a lawyer to argue, or present, a case before the Supreme Court. Hard work goes into preparing the case, which also includes long and detailed written arguments from both sides.

The Supreme Court convenes, or meets, the first Monday in October. It stays in session usually until late June of the next year. When they are not hearing cases, the Justices do legal research and write opinions. On Fridays, they meet in private — in "conference" — to discuss cases they've heard and to vote on them.

It takes a majority of Justices to decide a case. If the Chief Justice sides with the majority, he will write the majority opinion, or assign it to one of the other Justices on the majority side to write. If the Chief Justice is not in the majority, the most senior Justice—the one who has served on the court the longest—writes the opinion or assigns it to another Justice. These opinions are carefully worded since they become the basis upon which similar future cases are argued. Justices on the minority side are free to write dissenting, or differing, opinions.

Justices

The Supreme Court is made up of nine Justices, one of whom is the Chief Justice. They are appointed by the President and must be approved by the Senate. Once a person has been approved by the Senate and sworn in as a Supreme Court Justice, he or she remains in the job for life. The only way a Justice may leave the job is to resign, retire, die, or be impeached by the House and convicted by the Senate. No Justice has ever been removed by impeachment. There are no official qualifications in order to become a Justice, although all have been trained in the law and most pursued legal and political careers before serving on the Court. Several justices served as members of Congress, governors, or members of the Cabinet. One president, William Howard Taft, was later appointed Chief Justice.

The number of Supreme Court Justices has changed over the years. Initially, the Court was made up of six Justices who had been appointed by George Washington. The first time they met was February 1, 1790. The number of Justices has been as high as 10. President Franklin D. Roosevelt tried to raise the number to 15 at one point, but the number has been nine since 1869.

13

The Legislative Branch

The Congress of the United States was created by Article I, Section 1, of the Constitution, adopted by the Constitutional Convention on September 17, 1787, providing that *"All legislative Powers herein granted shall be vested in a Congress of the United States, which shall consist of a Senate and House of Representatives."* The first Congress under the Constitution met on March 4, 1789, in the Federal Hall in New York City.

The United States Congress is part of the legislative branch and is made up of two houses—the House of Representatives and the Senate. This two house system is known as a bicameal or two-part legislature. The primary duty of Congress is to write, debate, and pass bills, which are then passed on to the President for approval. Other congressional duties include investigating pressing national issues and supervising the executive and judicial branches.

Every two years, voters get to choose all 435 Representatives and a third of the Senators. The entire House membership faces re-election every two years, but the Senate is a continuing body because there is never an entirely new Senate. A new Congress begins in January following Congressional elections. Since the First Congress, which met from 1789 to 1791, all Congresses have been numbered in order. Congress meets once every year and usually lasts from January 3rd to July 31st, but in special cases, a session can last longer.

For the most part, the House and Senate each meet in their respective chamber in the US Capitol in Washington, DC. However, on rare occasions, they will convene for a joint session of Congress in the House chamber. For example, a joint session will be called to count electoral votes for presidential elections.

The Senate is composed of 100 Members, 2 from each State, who are elected to serve for a term of 6 years. Senators were originally chosen by the State legislatures. This procedure was changed by the 17th amendment to the Constitution, adopted in 1913, which made the election of Senators a function of the people. There are three classes of Senators, and a new class is elected every 2 years.

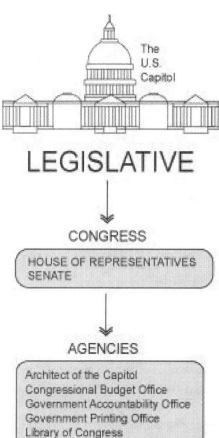

The U.S. Capitol

LEGISLATIVE

CONGRESS

HOUSE OF REPRESENTATIVES
SENATE

AGENCIES

Architect of the Capitol
Congressional Budget Office
Government Accountability Office
Government Printing Office
Library of Congress

Both the Senators and the Representatives must be residents of the State from which they are chosen. In addition, a Senator must be at least 30 years of age and must have been a citizen of the United States for at least 9 years; a Representative must be at least 25 years of age and must have been a citizen for at least 7 years.

A Resident Commissioner from Puerto Rico (elected for a 4-year term) and Delegates from American Samoa, the District of Columbia, Guam, and the Virgin Islands complete the composition of the Congress of the United States. Delegates are elected for a term of 2 years. The Resident Commissioner and Delegates may take part in the floor discussions but have no vote in the full House. They do, however, vote in the committees to which they are assigned and in the Committee of the Whole House on the State of the Union.

Powers of Congress

The Constitution grants Congress "all legislative powers" in the national government. Article I, Section 8, of the Constitution lists a wide range of congressional powers, including coining money, maintaining a military, declaring war on other countries, and regulating interstate and foreign commerce.

The Constitution states:

The Congress shall have Power to lay and collect Taxes, Duties, Imposts and Excises, to pay the Debts and provide for the common Defense and general Welfare of the United States; but all Duties, Imposts and Excises shall be uniform throughout the United States;

- To borrow money on the credit of the United States;

- To regulate Commerce with foreign Nations, and among the several States, and with the Indian Tribes;

- To establish an uniform Rule of Naturalization, and uniform Laws on the subject of Bankruptcies throughout the United States;

- To coin Money, regulate the Value thereof, and of foreign Coin, and fix the Standard of Weights and Measures;

- To provide for the Punishment of counterfeiting the Securities and current Coin of the United States;

- To establish Post Offices and Post Roads;

- To promote the Progress of Science and useful Arts, by securing for limited Times to Authors and Inventors the exclusive Right to their respective Writings and Discoveries;

- To constitute Tribunals inferior to the supreme Court;

- To define and punish Piracies and Felonies committed on the high Seas, and Offenses against the Law of Nations;

- To declare War, grant Letters of Marque and Reprisal, and make Rules concerning Captures on Land and Water;

- To raise and support Armies, but no Appropriation of Money to that Use shall be for a longer Term than two Years;

- To provide and maintain a Navy;

- To make Rules for the Government and Regulation of the land and naval Forces;

- To provide for calling forth the Militia to execute the Laws of the Union, suppress Insurrections and repel Invasions;

- To provide for organizing, arming, and disciplining the Militia, and for governing such Part of them as may be employed in the Service of the United States, reserving to the States respectively, the Appointment of the Officers, and the Authority of training the Militia according to the discipline prescribed by Congress;

- To exercise exclusive Legislation in all Cases whatsoever, over such District (not exceeding ten Miles square) as may, by Cession of particular States, and the acceptance of Congress, become the Seat of the

Government of the United States, and to exercise like
Authority over all Places purchased by the Consent of
the Legislature of the State in which the Same shall be,
for the Erection of Forts, Magazines, Arsenals, dock-
Yards, and other needful Buildings;

- To make all Laws which shall be necessary and proper
  for carrying into Execution the foregoing Powers, and
  all other Powers vested by this Constitution in the
  Government of the United States, or in any Department or Officer thereof.

Elastic Clause

Congress controls federal taxing and spending policies—one
of the most important sources of power in the government.
The Constitution gives Congress the authority to "make all
laws which shall be necessary and proper," an implied source
of power sometimes called the Elastic Clause.

One of the most important implied powers is Congress's
authority to investigate and oversee the executive branch
and its agencies, such as the Department of Defense and the
Department of Justice. As part of this responsibility, which is
known as oversight, Congress summons senior officials to answer questions from members, orders audits of agencies, and
holds hearings to air grievances of citizens.

Congress also holds hearings on matters of general public
concern. Sometimes members of Congress conduct these hearings to identify problems that create a need for new laws. In
other cases Congress holds hearings to raise public awareness
about an issue.

There are, however, some congressional powers that are
rarely used such as the ability to impeach an official and the
ability to amend the Constitution.

In addition to the power described above, Congress shares powers with the President in matters such as framing U.S. foreign policy and control over the military. For example, while the President negotiates treaties, they are only put into effect when the Senate approves them. Also, while Congress can declare war and approve funds for the military, the President is the commander-in-chief of the military.

Limits on Congress

Section 9 of Article I of the Constitution also imposes prohibitions upon Congress.

- The Migration or Importation of such Persons as any of the States now existing shall think proper to admit, shall not be prohibited by the Congress prior to the Year one thousand eight hundred and eight, but a tax or duty may be imposed on such Importation, not exceeding ten dollars for each Person.

- The privilege of the Writ of Habeas Corpus shall not be suspended, unless when in Cases of Rebellion or Invasion the public Safety may require it.

- No Bill of Attainder or *ex post facto* Law shall be passed.

- No capitation, or other direct, Tax shall be laid, unless in Proportion to the Census or Enumeration herein before directed to be taken. (Clarified by the 16th Amendment.)

- No Tax or Duty shall be laid on Articles exported from any State.

- No Preference shall be given by any Regulation of Commerce or Revenue to the Ports of one State over those of another: nor shall Vessels bound to, or from, one State, be obliged to enter, clear, or pay Duties in another.

- No Money shall be drawn from the Treasury, but in Consequence of Appropriations made by Law; and a regular Statement and Account of the Receipts and Expenditures of all public Money shall be published from time to time.

- No Title of Nobility shall be granted by the United States: And no Person holding any Office of Profit or Trust under them, shall, without the Consent of the Congress, accept of any present, Emolument, Office, or Title, of any kind whatever, from any King, Prince or foreign State.

Amending the Constitution

Another power vested in the Congress is the right to propose Amendments to the Constitution whenever two-thirds of both Houses shall deem it necessary. Should two-thirds of the State legislatures demand changes in the Constitution, it is the duty of Congress to call a Constitutional Convention. Proposed Amendments shall be valid as part of the Constitution when ratified by the legislatures or by conventions of three-fourths of the States, as one or the other mode of ratification may be proposed by Congress.

The Constitution states: *The Congress, whenever two thirds of both Houses shall deem it necessary, shall propose Amendments to this Constitution, or, on the Application of the Legislatures of two thirds of the several States, shall call a Convention for proposing Amendments, which, in either Case, shall be valid to all Intents and Purposes, as part of this Constitution, when ratified by the Legislatures of three fourths of the several States, or by Conventions in three fourths thereof, as the one or the other Mode of Ratification may be proposed by the Congress; Provided that no Amendment which may be made prior to the Year One thousand eight hundred and eight shall in any Manner affect the first and fourth Clauses in the Ninth Section of the first Article; and that no State, without its Consent, shall be deprived of its equal Suffrage in the Senate.*

Rights of Members

According to Section VI of Article I, Members of Congress are granted certain privileges. In no case, except in treason, felony, and breach of the peace, can members be arrested while attending sessions of Congress "and in going to and returning from the same. . . ." Furthermore, the members cannot be questioned in any other place for remarks made in Congress. Each House may expel a member of its body by a two-thirds vote.

Enactment of Laws

All bills and joint resolutions must pass both the House of Representatives and the Senate and then be signed by the President, except those proposing a Constitutional Amendment, in order to become law, or be passed over the President's veto by a two-thirds vote of both Houses of Congress. Section 7 of Article I states: *"If any Bill shall not be returned by the President within ten Days (Sundays excepted) after it shall have been presented to him, the Same shall be a Law, in like Manner as if he had signed it, unless the Congress by their Adjournment prevent its Return, in which Case it shall not be a Law."*

When a bill or joint resolution is introduced in the House, the usual procedure for its enactment into law is as follows:

- Assignment to House committee having jurisdiction;

- If favorably considered, it is reported to the House either in its original form or with recommended amendments;

- If the bill or resolution is passed by the House, it is messaged to the Senate and referred to the committee having jurisdiction;

- In the Senate committee the bill, if favorably considered, may be reported in the form as received from the House, or with recommended amendments;

- The approved bill or resolution is reported to the Senate, and if passed by that body, is returned to the House;

- If one body does not accept the amendments to a bill by the other body, a conference committee comprised of Members of both bodies is usually appointed to effect a compromise;

- When the bill or joint resolution is finally approved by both Houses, it is signed by the Speaker (or Speaker pro tempore) and the Vice President (or President pro tempore or acting President pro tempore) and is presented to the President; and

- Once the President's signature is affixed, the measure becomes a law. If the President vetoes the bill, it cannot become a law unless it is re-passed by a two-thirds vote of both Houses.

The House of Representatives

When the Constitution was being drafted, a debate broke out between States with large populations and those with smaller populations. Each had a different opinion about how the States should be represented in the new government. To be fair to each group, a compromise was reached. By dividing Congress into two houses, the House of Representatives would favor states with larger populations, while the Senate would favor those states with smaller populations.

There are a total of 435 members in the House of Representatives. Each member represents an area of a state, known as a Congressional District. The number of Representatives is based on the number of districts in a state. Each state is guaranteed one seat. Every ten years, the Census Bureau counts the population of the states to determine the number of districts in each state.

Representatives, elected for two-year terms, must be 25 years old, a citizen for at least seven years, and a resident of the state from which they are elected. Five additional members—from Puerto Rico, Guam, American Samoa, the Virgin Islands, and the District of Columbia—represent their constituencies in the House. While they may participate in the debates, they cannot vote.

The House has special jobs that only it can perform. It can:

- Start laws that make people pay taxes.

- Decide if a government official should be put on trial before the Senate if he or she has committed a crime against the country.

Powers of the House

The House of Representatives is granted the power of originating all bills for the raising of revenue. Both Houses of Congress act in impeachment proceedings, which, according to the Constitution, may be instituted against the President, Vice President, and all civil officers of the United States. The House of Representatives has the sole power of impeachment, and the Senate has the sole power to try impeachments.

The Senate

There are 100 members in the Senate. The Constitution states that the Vice President has formal control over the Senate and is known as the president of the Senate. In actuality, the Vice President is only present for important ceremonies and to cast a tie-breaking vote.

Senators, elected for six-year terms, must be 30 years old, a citizen for at least nine years, and a resident of the state from which they are elected. As in the House, the Senate also has special jobs that only it can perform. It can:

- Confirm or disapprove any treaties the President drafts.

- Confirm or disapprove the Presidential appointments, such as the Cabinet, officers, Supreme Court justices, and ambassadors.

- Holds a trial for a Government official who commits a crime against the country.

Powers of the Senate

Under the Constitution, the Senate is granted certain powers not accorded to the House of Representatives. The Senate approves or disapproves certain Presidential appointments by majority vote, and treaties must be concurred in by a two-thirds vote.

Committees

The work of preparing and considering legislation is done largely by committees of both Houses of Congress. There are 16 standing committees in the Senate and 19 in the House of Representatives. There are two select committees in each House and various congressional commissions and joint committees composed of Members of both Houses. Each House may also appoint special investigating committees. The membership of the standing committees of each House is chosen by a vote of the entire body; members of other committees are appointed under the provisions of the measure establishing them. Each bill and resolution is usually referred to the appropriate committee, which may report a bill out in its original form, favorably or unfavorably, recommend amendments, report original measures, or allow the proposed legislation to die in committee without action.

Part Three

Politics

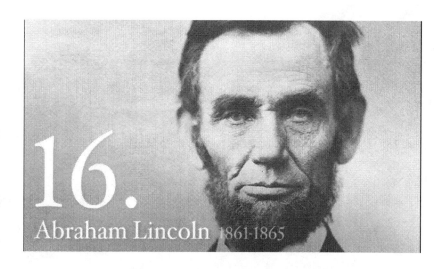

16.

Abraham Lincoln 1861-1865

What is conservatism?
Is it not the adherence to the old and tried
against the new and untried?

—Abraham Lincoln

The welfare of the people in particular has always been the alibi of tyrants.

—Albert Camus

In order to become the master, the politician poses as the servant.

—Charles de Gaulle

14

Individual Or Collective Rights

Roosevelt was among the most collectivist—anti-individual rights—Presidents the United States has ever had. In his 1944 State of the Union Address, President Franklin D. Roosevelt called for a "Second Bill of Rights," which included:

- The right to a useful and remunerative job in the industries or shops or farms or mines of the nation.

- The right to earn enough to provide adequate food and clothing and recreation.

- The right of every farmer to raise and sell his products at a return which will give him and his family a decent living.

- The right of every businessman, large and small, to trade in an atmosphere of freedom from unfair competition and domination by monopolies at home or abroad.

- The right of every family to a decent home.

- The right to adequate medical care and the opportunity to achieve and enjoy good health.

- The right to adequate protection from the economic fears of old age, sickness, accident and unemployment.

- The right to a good education.

These rights are very different from the rights Locke, Jefferson and the Founders had in mind when forming our government.

Obligates Others

Collective rights imply positive obligations on the part of others. When adequate food, clothing and recreation is a right, it does not mean that people have the right to work harder and longer so that they can afford to buy what they need. Rather it means that *other* people— employers, consumers, co-workers, taxpayers—are obligated to provide workers with wages sufficiently high to purchase these necessities.

> Collective rights imply positive obligations on the part of others.

The right of farmers to a decent living means *others* are obliged to insure that farmers have a minimum income. A right to a useful job actually means that *others* are obligated to provide that job if worker can't find one. A right to a home implies *others* are obligated to provide a home to those in need of housing.

Obligations Are Vague

How is the right to a decent job, for example, actually insured? Does the State assign workers to positions? What if the employer wants to hire someone else? Who decides? How can farmers be guaranteed a decent income? Are citizens required to purchase certain vegetables and fruits? At a certain price? What if you don't want to buy them? What if you can buy them elsewhere on sale? If you grow your own produce are you stepping on farmers rights? Who decides what is a decent job and a decent income, anyway? What if you want to make more?

> Collective rights transfer power to make even basic economic decisions from individuals to government.

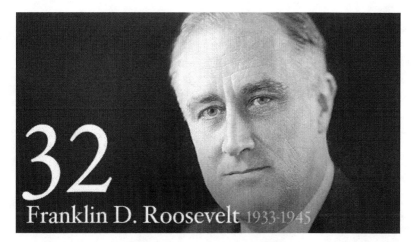

32
Franklin D. Roosevelt 1933-1945

Government Must Insure Rights

Roosevelt believed that everyone has the right to earn a decent income. Yet, every time you buy or sell something you would potentially violate one of Roosevelt's rights. By purchasing cherries to help one farmer, you deprive another by not buying his cherries. Fulfilling collective rights requires that all of us cede our freedom to the government when making economic decisions.

Unlimited Power Over Economy

Collective rights transfer power to make even basic economic decisions from individuals to government. The scope of government action in citizens' daily lives is enormous. Roosevelt believed that there was no economic decision—*no* act of buying, selling or producing—that government should not regulate. Roosevelt's Second Bill of Rights, like the rights delineated in the USSR Constitution, actually eliminate virtually all economic freedom of choice.

The 1977 USSR Constitution, for example, had 30 Articles describing the Rights that the State granted the People, including right to work, right to rest and leisure, to health protection, maintenance in old age, to housing, to education.

Rights Granted by the USSR Constitution

Article 40. Citizens of the USSR have the right to work . . .

Article 41. Citizens of the USSR have the right to rest and leisure. . .

Article 42. Citizens of the USSR have the right to health protection. . .

Article 43. Citizens of the USSR have the right to maintenance in old age, in sickness, and in the event of complete or partial disability or loss of the breadwinner.

Article 44. Citizens of the USSR have the right to housing.

Article 45. Citizens of the USSR have the right to education.

Collectivism

Collectivism refers to any moral, political, or social outlook that emphasizes the interdependence of every person in a collective group and the priority of group goals over individual goals. Collectivists focus on community and society, and give priority to group rights over individual rights.

How conservatives view human rights is quite different from progressive views. Progressives focus on human rights, equality, social justice, free elections—all of which sound great. But for progressives, rights are collective, not individual. This is an important distinction because there is little individual liberty in the collective.

For progressives, health care is as much of a "right" as the freedom to speak, worship, and assemble peacefully. What is ignored is that in every country where health care is guaranteed, that care is managed and rationed, doctors are limited, and the wait is long—all of which diminish freedom of the individual because buying care outside the system with one's own funds is prohibited—and unavailable.

Progressives say they believe in the right to free speech and free press and, yet, demand that conservative talk radio be curtailed, with many pressing for the return of the Fairness Doctrine to require radio stations "balance" their political talk shows, which would result in a suppression of conservative talk radio. Progressives want more regulation of guns and would have them all confiscated if they could do it. Progressive judges rule against expression of traditional Christian rituals, like Christmas and Easter, while claiming it is to protect religious freedom—by banishing it.

For progressives, such rights are "collective" to be controlled, rationed, restricted by the government to fit the "common good"—a concept introduced by Marx. For Marx, your value as an individual is defined by your contribution to the collective. When individual rights conflict with those of the collective, the collective's rights rule—for the common good. As you can see, Marxism and collective rights are hostile to individual liberty.

"Collectivism holds that the individual has no rights, that his life and work belong to the group (to "society," to the tribe, the state, the nation) and that the group may sacrifice him at its own whim to its own interests. The only way to implement a doctrine of that kind is by means of brute force—and statism has always been the political corollary of collectivism."

—Ayn Rand

Marxist-leaning progressives believe they have the right to redistribute your income and wealth, and eventually your property when it benefits the common good. Children are educated as the government sees fit. Parental rights? In California the powerful progressive-controlled Teachers Union nearly had home schooling outlawed. The loud outcry stopped the effort—temporarily. When you look closely you'll see a common thread—collective rights cede personal liberty to the State. Like FDR, they want a "living" Constitution and an "updated" Bill of Rights, which is actually a Bill of Needs. Progressives are elites who believe they—the State—know better than you do what you need, where they decide what you need, and how that need will be met.

For progressives, *the individual is dangerous*. Individuals think! Individuals step out of line and have differing notions from those of progressives who press for group-think. Individuals want to be unencumbered—less government, less regulation, more liberty. Individuals want to excel or fail by their abilities and to keep the rewards of their effort—not have it redistributed to those with greater need than their own. Conservatives believe, as the Founders did, that rights are not collective, or dependent upon the common good. For conservatives, our rights are natural rights endowed by a Creator, or the natural state of men. Conservatives see our rights as unalienable, not given to us by government.

Collectivism ideology underlies all totalitarian systems—socialism, communism, fascism, and Nazism alike. In collective society the group is above the individual, which allows that individual rights to be set aside with impunity, for the common good. Progressives—elitists who believe they know better what is best for the rest of us—promote, advocate, and enforce the centralization of all political power into an all-powerful central government, which they—the progressives—control.

Individualism

From the standpoint of Classical Realistic metaphysics, and as Aristotle noted, the Individual is the primary reality and has the first claim to recognition. Individuals are regarded as independent substances. In moral philosophy the ultimate end of human action is the free self-development of the individual that results in a life well-lived or happiness as conceived by Aristotle.

Society exists for the sake of the individual. The highest purpose of the State, if there is to be a State, consists in aiding individuals to achieve their own happiness. The result of this understanding of moral philosophy is that each individual, each human being, is supremely important. Each individual is an end in himself or herself and should regard his or her own success in life as of supreme importance.

> *"Individualism regards man—every man—as an independent, sovereign entity who possesses an unalienable right to his own life, a right derived from his nature as a rational being. Individualism holds that a civilized society, or any form of association, cooperation or peaceful co-existence among men, can be achieved only on the basis of the recognition of individual rights —and that a group, as such, has no rights other than the individual rights of its members."*

—Ayn Rand

In individualism, the state exists for the sake of the individual and not the individual for the sake of the state Anything that hints of "group-ness," whether it's unions, the public option, school lunches, social security, community organizing, even food stamps, is potentially a Trojan Horse sneaking the scourge of collectivism into our shining city on the hill.

To save America, we need more Madison and less Marx.

—Glenn Beck

*Our defense is in the preservation of the spirit
which prizes liberty as a heritage of all men,
in all lands, everywhere. Destroy this spirit
and you have planted the seeds of despotism
around your own doors.*

—Abraham Lincoln

15

Where Do You Stand Politically?

L iberal, Conservative, Right, Left, Libertarian? Where do you stand? Take this fun quiz and find out where you stand on The Political Map.

World's Smallest Political Quiz

Instructions: Read each statement one-by-one and consider if you agree or disagree with it. Circle the A when you *agree* with the statement. Circle the D when you *disagree* with the statement. Circle the M for *maybe* when you are *unsure* if you agree or disagree.

A. Personal Issues

1. Government should not censor speech,   A   M   D
   press, media or Internet.

2. Military service should be voluntary.   A   M   D
   There should be no draft.

3. There should be no laws regarding sex   A   M   D
   between consenting adults.

4. Laws prohibiting adult possession   A   M   D
   and use of drugs should be repealed.

5. There should be no National ID card.   A   M   D

B. Economic Issues

1. End "corporate welfare." No government   A   M   D
   handouts to business.
2. End government barriers to international   A   M   D
   free trade.
3. Let people control their own retirement: A   M   D
   Privatize Social Security.
4. Replace government welfare with   A   M   D
   private charity.
5. Cut taxes and government spending   A   M   D
   by 50% or more.

Scoring:

Starting with the statements under Personal Issues, count the number of A's circled and multiply that number by 20. Multiply the number of M's circled by 10; and multiply the number of D's by 0 (zero). Then, add the total of the A's, M's and D's to get your PI score. Repeat the same process to obtain your Economic Issues (EI) score. (Note: for both issues, the highest possible score is 100 and the lowest is 0.)

Write your scores below:

PI score _____ Personal Issues
EI score _____ Economic Issues

Plot Your Position

Looking at The Political Map (page 99), notice the line on the bottom left just above "Personal Issues Score" going from 0 (zero) to 100. Place an "X" where your PI score falls along this line. Next, put an "X" where your EI score lies on the line that goes from 0 (zero) to 100 on the lower-right side of the Map, just above "Economic Issues Score", Then going out from each mark, follow the grid lines until they meet. Circle this intersection point.

The intersection point is where you stand—your political position. This is not a fixed position, rather the Quiz measures *tendencies, not absolutes.* Your score shows who most agrees with you in politics, and where you agree and disagree with other political philosophies.

The Political Map

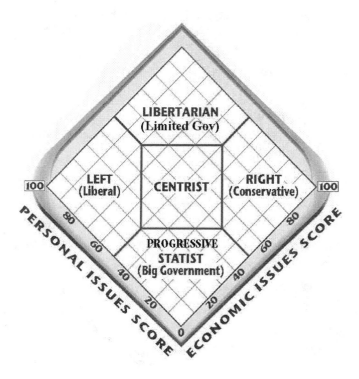

For years, politics has been represented as one-dimensional, a choice between left (or liberal) and right (or conservative). Growing numbers of thinkers agree this is far too narrow a view—and excludes millions of people. The Political Map is two-dimensional, which gives a more accurate representation of the true, diverse political world.

Political Philosophies

Libertarians support a great deal of liberty and freedom of choice in both personal and economic matters. They believe government's only purpose is to protect people from coercion and violence. They value individual responsibility, and tolerate economic and social diversity.

Left-Liberals generally embrace feelings of choice in personal matters, but support central decision-making in economics. They want the government to help the disadvantaged in the name of fairness. Leftists tolerate social diversity, but work for what might be described as "economic equality."

Right-Conservatives favor freedom of choice on economic issues, but want official standards in personal matters. They tend to support the free market, but frequently want the government to defend the community from what they see as threats to morality or to traditional family structure.

Centrists favor selective government intervention and emphasize what they commonly describe as "practical solutions" to current problems. They tend to keep an open mind on political issues. Many centrists feel that government serves as a check on excessive liberty.

Statists want government to have a great deal of control over individuals and society. They support centralized planning, and often doubt whether liberty and freedom of choice are practical options. At the very bottom of The Political Map, left-authoritarians are usually called "socialists", while right-authoritarians are generally called "fascists".

CREDIT:

The "World's Smallest Political Quiz" chart, political map, and description of political philosophies at the beginning of the chapter are based upon the work of David Nolan, cofounder of the Libertarian Party and reprinted by permission. Copyright by Advocates for Self-Government, 269 Market Place Blvd., #106, Cartersville, GA 30121-2235, 800-932-1776, Email: Quiz@TheAdvocates.org., Fax: 770-386-8373.

Web: www.TheAdvocates.org.

16

Conservative v. Liberal Views

M ost of us want the same things—freedom, prosperity; a healthy family, opportunity to be the best we can be; crime-free streets. How to create these conditions is where we differ. We tend to think of two general camps: Conservatives on the right and Liberal on the left. Of course, these are artificial boxes. We may be a little to the left on one issue and a little to the right on another because we are individuals, after all. So we don't fit readily into a box. And we learned from The Political Map, in the last chapter, that small v. large government is an important variable. Still, it is helpful to separate out the two views to get a better understanding of each.

Liberal and conservative beliefs tend to be complete opposites of each other. Conservatives look to traditional American values of personal responsibility, self-reliance, individual liberty and limited government, free markets, and strong national defense. Conservative policies aim to empower the individual to pursue happiness, and to keep government in check so that people have the freedom to pursue their own goals.

By contrast, Liberals place high value on tolerance and equality for all. They believe that the State should act to protect civil liberties and to alleviate social ills. Liberal beliefs are considered to have progressive views of the future; whereas conservative beliefs are viewed as being traditional.

Family and Marriage

The traditional family unit is highly valued by conservatives because it is the basic building block of society's institutions and weaves the very fabric of cultural values. They believe that marriage should take place between a man and a woman and support programs that promote moral behavior. Conservatives favor tradition and generally suspect things that fall outside traditional views of "normal."

Liberals believe individuals should be tolerant and respectful of differences. Economic realities force mothers out of the home and into the work place. Divorced parents, unwed mothers and adopting homosexuals have changed the portrait of parenthood—there is no "typical" family and the traditional stereotype of a nuclear unit is no longer applicable. Definitions of family and marriage must be expanded to include non-traditional family units, including homosexual unions and gay marriage. A liberal view is one that is open to re-defining "normal."

Role of Government

Conservatives value individual responsibility and resist government intervention. They believe power should remain with the states and the people, whereas liberals believe that power should reside in a strong central government. Conservatives reject the view that it is the job of the government to solve the problems of society by imposing intrusive policies, such as affirmative action or mandatory health care programs. Conservatives favor a limited role for government, with a small budget. They believe individuals should retain more of their own earnings and pay less to the government, whereas liberals believe that taxes are a costly but necessary evil and see conservatives as selfish and uncaring.

Conservatives don't like big government, with lots of procedures and social programs that clot up the system and aren't as effective as a free market economy. Liberals believe that it is the role of government to take responsibility for fixing the social injustices because government is the only force strong enough to bring about fairness—called "social justice"—to the people. Affirmative action within the workforce and educational system was designed to give minorities and women extra help in going to particular colleges and getting a job.

Liberals push for legal protections to avoid the conviction of innocent persons in the criminal justice system, reasonable restraints on government surveillance of American citizens, and fair procedures to ensure that alleged enemy combatants are in fact enemy combatants.

Government Programs

Liberals believe that prejudice and stereotyping in society hamper the opportunities for disadvantaged citizens. Government must respect and affirmatively safeguard the liberty, equality and dignity of each individual. They push for government-funded programs as the best way to address inequalities—derived from historical discrimination.

> For conservatives, government must respect and affirmatively safeguard the liberty, equality and dignity of *each* individual.

Terms such as "bleeding hearts" and "tax and spenders" refer to liberal public policies that address perceived unfair access to health care, housing, and jobs.

Liberals champion the rights of racial, religious, and ethnic minorities, political dissidents, persons accused of crime, and the outcasts of society. Liberals have established the right to counsel, a broad application of the right to due process of law, and the principle of equal protection for all people.

Conservatives believe in pulling yourself up by your own bootstraps. They see social programs as little more than giving handouts to people who should be working. For liberals, government has a fundamental responsibility to help those who are less fortunate. They support robust government programs to improve health care, education, social security, job training, and welfare for the neediest members of society. America is a national community, like a big family, and government exists in part to promote the general welfare.

For liberals, government has a fundamental responsibility to *help* those who are less fortunate.

National Defense

Conservatives advocate a strong national defense with the military providing security for society. They believe that a large military presence is an essential tool for safeguarding society against acts of terrorism.

By contrast, liberals believe government must protect the safety and security of the people but that war is to be avoided and emphasize negotiation for safeguarding society, in lieu of amassing armaments and soldiers. For liberals, communication with our enemies and understanding their priorities is the surest means of safeguarding society. Because liberals respect competing values, such as procedural fairness and individual dignity, they weigh more carefully particular exercises of government power, such as the use of secret evidence, hearsay, and torture.

Faith and Religion

Conservatives support laws that promote ethics and morality, based on values founded in a strong Judeo-Christian heritage. Liberals believe that moral and ethical behavior should be discovered by each individual through self-reflection rather than looking to Judeo-Christian heritage. Liberals believe church and state should be separate and that religion has no place in politics or governmental activities. More left-leaning liberals, or progressives, want the word "God" removed from government work-related events. Liberals oppose school prayer and teaching creationism in public schools.

The debate about assisted suicide illustrates the different views. Conservatives believe that "Thou shalt not kill" is a pretty straightforward statement, and that it is immoral to kill a person to end his or her suffering. Liberals, on the other hand, believe that people should be able to end their own life or the life of a loved one under some circumstances, especially under extreme conditions of suffering.

Right to Life

Conservatives and liberals agree that murder is wrong and that government shouldn't be allowed to interfere in private medical decisions. Their views on abortion differ dramatically, however. Conservatives, and especially Christian conservatives, express strong feelings about the sanctity of life. Human life begins at conception, and, because they cherish human life, conservatives oppose abortion. Liberals generally support a woman's right to control her body and her destiny. They do not think that human life begins at conception and believe abortion should be legal and women should be allowed to choose whether or not to carry a child to birth.

Death Penalty

Liberals want to abolish the death penalty because it is a cruel and unusual punishment no matter what the circumstances of their crime. Conservatives, on the other hand, believe the death penalty a just punishment for certain crimes.

Role of the Courts

Liberals believe courts have a responsibility to protect individual liberties. Rulings of liberal judges have preserved and continue to preserve freedom of expression, individual privacy, freedom of religion, and due process of law. Conservatives see liberal judges as using the bench to create rights which they say is "legislating from the bench". Conservative judges tend to use judicial authority to strengthen the Constitution, and to protect property rights and the interests of corporations.

Constitution

Conservatives are concerned about preserving the Constitution whereas liberals, especially progressive liberals, see the Constitution as antiquated and an impediment. They want a "living Constitution" that adapts to the issues of the time. Conservatives see the living Constitution as nothing more than a desire to eliminate the protections it affords individuals.

Summary

The most familiar and influential national party for liberals is the Democratic Party; whereas conservatives generally support the Republican Party. Conservatives also support the Libertarian Party.

There are different levels of liberalism. The more radical liberal beliefs a person has, the more likely they agree with these ideas and call themselves "progressive". Some liberal beliefs are more progressive than others. Another political party, the Socialist Party, operates from an extremely liberal viewpoint. The Republican Party and the Independent Party operates from more conservative viewpoints.

Conservative	Liberal
Abortion:	
Human life begins at conception. Abortion is murder.	Fetus is not a human life. Abortion is woman's personal choice and government should stay out of it
Affirmative Action:	
Admission and hiring should be based on ability.	Minorities lag behind whites due to discrimination. Affirmative action is needed to alleviate this injustice
Death Penalty:	
Support the death penalty. Punishment should fit the crime.	The death penalty is inhumane should be abolished. An execution is a State murder.

Conservative	Liberal

Welfare:
Oppose long-term welfare because it is more effective to encourage a person to become self-reliant, than keeping them dependent on the government. We need to provide opportunities to make it possible for poor and low-income workers to become self-reliant.

Support welfare. We need welfare to provide for the poor. Welfare brings fairness to American economic life. Without welfare, life below the poverty line would be intolerable.

Economy:

The free market system, competitive capitalism, and private enterprise produce more economic growth, more jobs and higher standards of living than those systems burdened by excessive government regulation.

Capitalism encourages greed. Government regulation is needed to protect people from abuses of big businesses.

Competition

Motivated by self interest

Social justice

Motivated by public interest

Role of Government:

Need accountability

Insure equal opportunity

Separation of powers

States rights

Regulation needed

Fix inequality; social justice.

Centralized power

Education:

Support school vouchers because parents should decide how and where to educate their child.

Need to fund existing public schools, raise teacher salaries, and reduce class size. School vouchers programs are untested.

Conservative	Liberal
Environment: Extreme environmental policies destroy jobs and damage the economy. Let competition in private sector bring green conditions. Skeptical about climate change claims.	Humans cause climate change, which harms the environment, threatens our health, and leads to species extinction. The government must regulate to protect the environment even if it causes some job losses and increased prices.
Gun Control: The 2nd Amendment gives the individual the right to keep and bear arms. Gun control laws do not thwart criminals. You have a right to defend yourself against criminals. More guns mean less crime.	The 2nd Amendment gives no individual the right to own a gun, but allows the State to keep a militia, like the National Guard. Guns kill.
Taxes: Support lower taxes and a small government. Lower taxes create incentives to work, save, invest, and engage in enterprise. Money is best spent by those who earn it.	Support higher taxes and a larger government. High taxes enable the government to do good and create jobs. We need high taxes for social welfare programs, to provide for the poor. We can't afford to cut taxes.
War on Terror: The militant Islamist utopia cannot peacefully co-exist with the Western world. Terrorism must be stopped and terrorists destroyed.	9/11 was caused by America's arrogant foreign policy. America needs to stop angering other countries. The threat posed by terrorism has been exaggerated for political advantage.

Conservative	Liberal

Health Care:

Free health care provided by the government is socialized medicine and means that everyone will get the same poor-quality health care. Health care should remain privatized.

Support universal government-supervised health care. There are millions of Americans who can't afford health insurance. They are being deprived of a basic right to health care.

Immigration:

Support legal immigration, oppose illegal immigration and amnesty. Government should enforce immigration laws. Illegals have broken the law and should not have the same rights as those who obey the law by entering legally.

If there were a decrease in cheap, illegal immigrant labor, employers would have to substitute higher-priced domestic employees, legal immigrants, or perhaps increase mechanization

Illegals are taking jobs from legal citizens

Support legal immigration and increasing the number of legal immigrants. Support blanket amnesty for illegal immigrants.

Believe that regardless of how they came to the U.S., illegal immigrants deserve:
- financial aid for college tuition.
- visas for spouse/children because families shouldn't be separated.

Illegal immigrants do the jobs that Americans do not want to do.

If you protest from the left, it is romanticized; if you protest from the right, you are demonized.

—Greg Gutfelt

Conservative	Liberal

United Nations:

The UN has repeatedly failed in its essential mission—to preserve world peace. History shows that the United States, not the UN, is the global force for spreading freedom, prosperity, tolerance and peace. The U.S. should never subvert its national interests to those of the UN.

The U.S. has a moral and a legal obligation to support the U.N. The UN can be effective in promoting peace and human rights. The U.S. should not have acted in Iraq without UN approval. The U.S. should submit its national interests to the greater good, as defined by the UN.

Religion:

The phrase "separation of church and state" is not in the Constitution. The 1st Amendment to the Constitution states "Congress shall make no law respecting an establishment of religion, or prohibiting the free exercise thereof..." This prevents the government from establishing a national church, but it does not prohibit God from being acknowledged in schools and government buildings.

Support the separation of church and state. Religious expression has no place in government.

Oppose the removal of symbols of Christian heritage from public and government spaces.

Support the removal of all references to God in public and government spaces.

Government should not interfere with religion and religious freedom.

Religion should not interfere with government.

17

What is Progressivism?

Progressivism is a popular reform effort that began in the late 1880s that seeks to "re-found" America. Progressives repudiate the Founder's belief in the existence of self-evident truths. They claim man enjoys no permanent rights endowed by God, only changing rights held at the indulgence of government.

The intellectual, cultural and political elites have blithely abandoned the principles of America's founding as outdated, defective, and of little relevance to modern governance. A visually annoyed House Speaker Nancy Pelosi, snorted "Are you serious?!" to a reporter who asked where in the Constitution was Congress granted authority to require citizens to buy health care insurance. Progressives promote a Constitution that endlessly evolves and adapts to the times because there are no eternal truths or permanent rights — everything is relative.

At its core Progressivism denies the existence of God and therefore the existence of eternal verities and objective standards of right and wrong — standards embodied in the Judeo-Christian tradition upon which the Founding Fathers constructed the framework of America. Progressives believe the end — utopia on earth through enlightened government that fundamentally changes human nature — justifies whatever means must be employed to attain it.

The Progressive Movement took root under Theodore Roosevelt, a Republican president, and was championed by Woodrow Wilson, a Democrat, who set forth a platform of a liberal government mandated to engineer a better society, assure equal outcomes, and redistribute wealth. The New Deal—President Franklin Roosevelt—and the Great Society—President Lyndon Johnson—were giant steps toward achieving the Progressive Platform. Progressives insist the modern world is so complex and problematic that we need an activist government to manage political life and human affairs. President Barack Obama and his Congress aggressively pressed a Progressive Agenda.

Progressives seek to transform our Constitutional structure of limited government into an all-powerful, centralized government focused on social reform, social justice—fairness. The American idea of self-government is being undercut by the rise of the modern administrative state, the growth of bureaucracy at every level, and the host of benefits the public has come to expect from government.

> *They know the answer is more government, they just don't know what the question is.*
>
> —Newt Gingrich

Progressives advocate for a new economic order, something different from both capitalism and communism. Progressives argue that an activist government should exercise economic sovereignty and engage in economic planning to

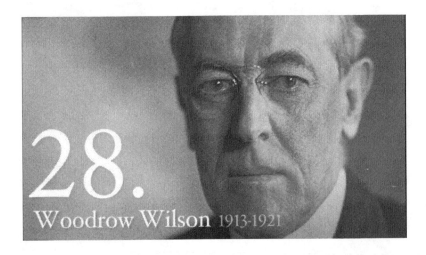

28. Woodrow Wilson 1913-1921

regulate, nationalize—even abolish private corporations as they decide. They seek to bring in a world in which cooperation replaces competition as the guiding rule of the economy; in which human values reign over those of the market; and in which sweeping inequality is replaced by redistribution of wealth. They promise that everyone will have "a fair share in national prosperity".

Progressives put faith in collective action and believe the flaws in society created by humans can be fixed by humans. The vision they put forward is of economic sovereignty—the right to decide how each one of us lives our lives in the workplace, in the marketplace, and in the public square—must be taken from the hands of monopolistic corporations and restored to popular government.

Historians and many economists praise Progressivism and its results, with the exception of prohibition. Passage of antitrust laws is an example of "progress". History texts, encyclopedias, and news stories tell how huge business trusts were monopolizing the economy, artificially driving up prices, producing shoddy products, and generally dragging down the standard of living for most people. Progressives passed aggressive enforcement of antitrust laws that broke up many trusts and set the stage for prosperity. Economic prospects for nearly everyone increased by the end of the 19th Century, as prices for goods fell.

The wedding of mainstream journalism and statism is an insidious relationship from the Progressive Era when formerly independent journalists became a drumbeat for expansion of the power of the state. Today the media is heavily biased towards Progressive views.

Not Just Dems
Both Republicans and Democrats can be progressive. They tend to be elitist, disdaining voters who they view as ignorant. They prefer government-by-experts. Contrary to what one

would expect, many have been ethnocentric, even outright racist, seeing immigrants and blacks as lesser races in need of guidance. Woodrow Wilson thought so when he segregated the federal government and Theodore Roosevelt largely agreed when it came to the invasion of the Philippines or military interventions into Latin America. The Progressive Era was also the era when Jim Crow was established in law through the active disenfranchisement of blacks and poor whites, and the era of race riots.

Progressives have used the Amendment process to re-work the Constitution. Passage of the 16th, 17th, 18th and 19th Amendments greatly expanded the scope of the central government—a primary goal of Progressives. The 16th Amendment authorized Congress to levy an income tax. The 17th Amendment gave the power of appointment of Senators to voters, which helped make the states subservient to the national agenda of Progressives. The 18th Amendment was prohibition of alcoholic beverages and the 19th Amendment forced all states to grant women the right to vote.

Imposition of the income tax with the 16th Amendment gave a green light for unchecked growth of the central government. Prohibition further increased the power of the central government over the property of Americans, while 17th Amendment altered the delicate balance of powers laid by the Founders.

As government expands, liberty contracts.
—Ronald Reagan

Progressivism led to the Great Depression and Franklin Roosevelt's expansion of the powers of the state prolonged it. But Progressives convinced the public that the solution to the economic downturn was to further expand government and spending.

In the Progressive view, only those educated in the favored top universities, preferably in the social sciences, are believed to be capable of governing. Politics is too complex for common sense. Only government agencies staffed by experts can manage tasks previously handled within the private sphere. The Founders, on the other hand, thought that laws should be made by a body of elected officials with roots in local communities, not by experts.

I would rather be governed by the first two thousand people in the Boston telephone directory than by the two thousand people on the faculty at Harvard.

—William F. Buckley, Jr.

The Founders rejected the idea of a permanent political class, which is what we have running government today. The traditional view of politics, stemming from the idea that the ordinary citizen would lay down their implements, go serve for a time in their government is viewed by Progressives as naïve and folksy.

Progressives want people to take power out of the hands of locally elected officials and political parties and place it into the hands of the central government, which will establish administrative agencies run by neutral experts, scientifically trained, to translate the people's inchoate will into concrete policies—because we common folks are too stupid to govern ourselves—the exact opposite of what our Founds knew to be right.

Progressives v. Liberals

Liberals believe that taxpayer dollars can help individuals afford bare necessities and entice institutions to support the common good. Progressive focuses on using the government's treasury as a means to ends, whether those ends are better health care—Medicare, stronger job growth—tax credits, or more robust export businesses—corporate subsidies.

Economic Progressivism believes the government is the best instrument of social change—food safety, minimum wage and labor laws, as well as post-depression financial rules and enforcement agencies. As the nation's supreme authority, the government should set parameters channeling capitalism's profit motive into societal priorities and keeping that profit motive under control.

A liberal solution to high energy costs would be to increase funding for particular social programs; whereas a Progressive solution would be to crack down on price gouging and pass laws better-regulating the particular industry's profiteering and market manipulation tactics. A liberal policy towards prescription drugs is to give a lot of taxpayer cash to the pharmaceutical industry for them to provide medicine to the poor; while Progressive prescription drug policy would be to regulate prices and bulk purchasing to force down the actual cost of medicine.

Progressives are pushing America toward European-style centralization of power. They want a highly regulated economy, nationalization of industries and socialized health care, with lawmakers leaving the implementation to *unelected* bureaucrats. While Progressives say this is progress, it is actually the revival of a failed, undemocratic and oppressive kind of statism.

Good intentions will always be pleaded for every assumption of authority. It is hardly too strong to say that the Constitution was made to guard the people against the dangers of good intentions. There are men in all ages who mean to govern well, but they mean to govern. They promise to be good masters, but they mean to be masters.

—Daniel Webster

Part Four

Dangers

*From each according to his ability,
to each according to his need.*

—Karl Marx

Naomi Wolf outlines 10 steps necessary for a fascistic government to destroy the democratic character of a nation-state and subvert the social/political liberty previously exercised by its citizens.

1. Invoke a terrifying internal and external enemy.

2. Create secret prisons where torture takes place.

3. Develop a thug caste or paramilitary force not answerable to citizens.

4. Set up an internal surveillance system.

5. Harass citizens' groups.

6. Engage in arbitrary detention and release.

7. Target key individuals.

8. Control the press.

9. Treat all political dissidents as traitors.

10. Suspend the rule of law.

—Naomi Wolf
In The End of America
A Letter of Warning to a Young Patriot

18

Cycle of Democracy

M any incorrectly believe that the United States is a democracy or majority rule, but they are mistaken. The United States is a republic, which is characterized by the rule of law. Democracies—sometimes called mob rule—are an unstable form of government. The Founders understood this. They designed the legislature to give the people representation, but the legislature is limited by the rules of the Constitution, which is designed to be very difficult to change through the laborious Amendment process. Our strict Constitution is the only thing between us and the mob rule of pure democracy.

Democracy sounds good in theory, but just because the majority agrees, doesn't make it fair or just—or even smart! Consider lynch mobs. The majority convicts and executes. This is all fine if you are in the majority. What if you are in the minority? Suppose the majority decides to give your home to someone they think deserves it more than you do. Majority-rule communities can devolve into a kind of Lord-of-the-Flies dynamic. The flaw in democracy is that the majority is unrestrained. When more than half the people are persuaded to want something, they rule. Majorities can become an unruly, abusive mob trampling the rights of the minority.

Rule of Law

A republic is ruled by law, where the government is limited by law, leaving the people alone. The Founders chose to give us the rule of law in a republic and not rule of the majority in a democracy. In a republic, rather than being lynched by a mob, people charged with crimes have rights, including a trial by a jury of peers. Republics offer more protection of the individual rights of *all* of its citizens, not just those in the majority.

Governments are dynamic; they evolve and change. A leader with an agenda to push may look longingly at majority rule such as when President Obama argued the fairness of a 51% vote to pass the controversial Reconciliation Bill that put the Senate version of Obamacare into law—when it would have taken a 60% vote in the Senate. "It's only *fair*," he insisted as a bill opposed by the majority of Americans barely squeaked through the House. Obama would be delighted if bills could get through the then-democratic-controlled Senate with 51%, which would allow quick passage of many controversial programs resisted by the minority. Keep in mind that 49% puts a group into the minority. With approximately 300 million people in the country, this means that bills opposed by some 147,000,000 people—49%—could go into law.

Maintaining a republic takes constant vigilance because power hungry politicians will press towards majority votes. It's only "fair" after all. Ben Franklin well-understood this when at the close of the Constitutional Convention of 1787, he was asked by a woman, "What have you given us?" To which he replied, "A republic, Ma'am, if you can keep it." This is the challenge. Today many patriots fear that we are losing our republic and sliding into a democracy—or worse!

The Founders wanted to keep us from having a democracy. The word "democracy" does not appear in the Declaration of Independence or the U.S. Constitution or in any of the Constitutions of the fifty states.

Unstable

Besides democracy's propensity toward extremes, with possible unfairness and abuse towards the minority, it is an unstable form of government. Alexander Hamilton observed, "Real liberty is never found in despotism or in the extremes of democracy." Another of the Founders, James Madison wrote in *The*

Federalist Papers, "Democracies have ever been spectacles of turbulence and contention, have ever been found incompatible with personal security or the rights of property and have in general been as short in their lives as they have been violent in their deaths." Samuel Adams noted, "Democracy never lasts long. It soon wastes, exhausts, and murders itself."

The Founders knew history. They knew that democracies in the early Greek city states produced wild excesses of government, which in every case evolved into mob rule, then anarchy, and finally tyranny under an oligarchy.

Looking back at the Roman Empire we see the same evolution that seems to be happening in early 21st century America. Initially the Romans set out Roman law and built a republic with limited government power. People were free to produce and could keep the fruits of their labor. Romans, like Americans, became wealthy and forgot that as government power grows, freedom declines. Roman citizens grew complacent as power-hungry politicians increasingly exceeded the powers granted them in the Roman Constitution—just as they have done in America. Roman politicians used government power to take private property, which they gave to others.

As the Roman politicians granted agriculture subsidies, housing and welfare programs, taxes rose along with imposition of controls over the private sector. Increasingly productive citizen went on the public dole. Inevitably, productivity dropped, shortages developed, and mobs demanded food and services from the government. Eventually the system came crashing down. The Roman Empire devolved from a republic to a democracy to an oligarchy with a progression of Caesars.

About the time the Constitution was adopted in 1787, Alexander Tyler, a Scottish history professor at the University of Edinburgh, agreed with the Founders that a democracy is always temporary in nature. He worried that America may make the same mistakes that lead to the fall of the Athenian Republic 2000 years earlier.

Tyler's insight was that democracy cannot exist as a permanent form of government. When voters discover they can vote themselves generous gifts from the public treasury the majority will thereafter vote for the candidates who promise to deliver the most benefits from the public pool—other people's money. This is what lead to the demise of the Athenian Republic and the Roman Empire. Such de-evolution of democracy occurred across Europe—Portugal, Ireland, Greece, Spain—in the early 21st Century. Tyler asserted that every democracy eventually collapses from loose fiscal policy—always followed by a dictatorship.

The Tyler Cycle of Democracy

The average age of the world's greatest civilizations from the beginning of history, has been about 200 years. During those 200 years, these nations always progressed through the following sequence:

1. From bondage to spiritual faith;

2. From spiritual faith to great courage;

3. From courage to liberty;

4. From liberty to abundance;

5. From abundance to complacency;

6. From complacency to apathy;

7. From apathy to dependence;

8. From dependence back into bondage

—Alexander Tyler

The federal government continues to spend more money than it takes in, unlike local governments, which are forced to adhere to a fixed budget. This is translating to more government control in all aspects of our lives, which means less individual freedom as we accept more government handouts, requiring more taxation. America is sliding down the slippery slope of apathy into dependency.

A democracy cannot sustain itself because the voting public votes for their own best interests rather than for the best interest of the country. Politicians care only about getting re-elected, which they do by bringing home the bacon for their state, instead of insisting upon sound fiscal policy across the board. Taxes are used to maintain dependency on the federal government and protect the incumbency of politicians, instead of using tax dollars wisely to maintain infrastructure and protect our individual freedom.

Patriots know that the downfall of America is inevitable if we continue on this path. Dependency on the ever-growing federal government is leading us into bondage. Just as it happened in Rome, so, too, will we enslave ourselves by our own greed.

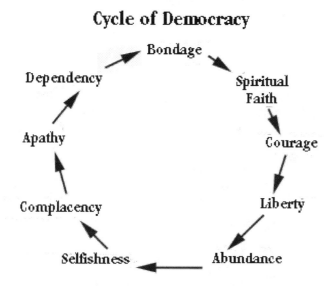

Cycle of Democracy

Reliance on government leads to the growth of government, which leads to the dominance of government, which leads to bondage to government.

— Bret Burquest

With some 47% percent of the nation's population paying
no income tax, Professor Joseph Olson of Hamline University
School of Law believes the United States is now somewhere
between the complacency and apathy phase of Tyler's cycle
of democracy—moving rapidly towards the governmental
dependency phase.

Thus, if not diligently maintained, democracy tends to
gradually evolve from limited government to the total rule of
an oligarchy. We Americans have two choices—restore our
republic or we will surely end up under the tyranny of an elite
oligarchy.

America will never be destroyed from the outside.
If we falter and lose our freedoms,
it will be because we destroyed ourselves.

—Abraham Lincoln

19

Crisis Strategy

O rchestrated crisis is a powerful subversive strategy for forcing political change. It was first proposed in 1966 by Columbia University political scientists Richard Andrew Cloward and Frances Fox Piven who created a plan to bankrupt the welfare as a means to produce radical social change. The Cloward-Piven approach called for swamping the welfare rolls with new applicants—more than the system could bear—with the goal of causing its economic collapse to lead to political turmoil and ultimately to socialism.

Cloward and Piven charged that the ruling classes used welfare to silence the poor by providing a social safety net to douse the possibility of rebellion. Cloward had the insight that poor people can advance only when "the rest of society is afraid of them". Activists should work to sabotage and destroy the welfare system instead of placating the poor with government handouts. The collapse of the welfare state would ignite a political and financial crisis that would rock the nation when poor people rise in revolt.

Cloward and Piven called for "cadres of aggressive organizers" to use "demonstrations to create a climate of militancy." Intimidated, politicians would appeal to the federal government for help. Media campaigns would promote a federal program of income redistribution in the form of a guaranteed living income for all—working and non-working both. Terrified by the crisis, local officials would apply pressure on Washington to implement it. With every major city erupting into chaos, Washington would have to act.

Fundamentally Transforming American

Cloward and Piven provided a blueprint for the transformation of America through the fall of capitalism by overloading the government bureaucracy with a flood of impossible demands, thus pushing society into crisis and economic collapse.

Cloward and Piven counseled activists to create Trojan Horse movements whose outward purpose is providing material help to the downtrodden while the actual purpose is to mobilize poor people en masse to overwhelm government agencies with a flood of demands beyond the capacity of those agencies to meet. The flood of demands is calculated to break the budget, jam the bureaucratic gears into gridlock, and bring the system crashing down. Fear, turmoil, violence and economic collapse will accompany such a breakdown—providing perfect conditions for fostering radical change.

Create Crisis to Drive Change

By 2010 it seemed increasingly apparent that the Obama Administration was implementing the Cloward-Piven strategy on an unprecedented scale by flooding America with a tidal wave of poisonous initiatives, orders, regulations, and laws. As Rahm Emanuel, White House Chief of Staff, said, "A crisis is a terrible thing to waste."

> A crisis is a terrible thing to waste.
> —Rahm Emanuel

The *real* goal of "health care" legislation, the *real* goal of "cap-and-trade," and the *real* goal of the "stimulus" was to rip out the heart of private economy and transfer it to the government to control. With passage of the Financial Reform Bill the government gained control over 70% of the US economy. These initiatives were vehicles of change—transformation of America into something we may not recognize. Their purpose was to deliver power. Each of these massive spending bill made the economic situation much worse—*which was their purpose.*

In addition to overwhelming the government with demands for services, Obama and the Democrats are overwhelming political opposition to their plans with a flood of apocalyptic legislation with the goal of leaving the American people discouraged, demoralized, and exhausted.

The policies are unconstitutional—*deliberately so*—because the objective is to make the Constitution irrelevant. Government spending is off the charts, driving us into hyperinflation. The policies are toxic. The ideologies are poisonous and yet they are enacted into law—laws the legislatures hadn't even read when voting.

I apprehend no danger to our country from a foreign foe. Our destruction, should it come at all, will be from another quarter, from the inattention of the people to the concerns of their government. From their carelessness and negligence I must confess that I do apprehend some danger. I fear that they may place too implicit a confidence in their public servants and fail properly to scrutinize their conduct. That in this way may be made the dupes of designing men and become the instruments of their own undoing. Make them intelligent and they will be vigilant. Give them the means of detecting the wrong and they will apply the remedy.

—Daniel Webster

20

How to Destroy American

A merica is great nation created from peoples of all nations in the world. In the 20th century when our immigration laws were still enforced–assimilation worked and made the swift attainment of the American Dream possible for millions of immigrants seeking to escape deplorable conditions. It was expressed in our motto–*E pluribus unum: Out of many, one.*

A diverse, peaceful, stable society is a rarity and generally short-lived because diverse people tend to have considerable animosity towards those who are different from them. We need unity to keep a nation together. Ancient Greece is an example. The Greeks had one language and a common literature, they worshiped the same god and belonged to the same race. They had a common enemy—Persia. Despite these bonds local patriotism and geographical conditions promoted political divisions and Greece fell.

Former Colorado Governor Richard D. Lamm identified eight steps towards the destruction of the United States.

1. *Turn America into a bilingual or multi-lingual, bicultural country.*

   Bilingual and bicultural societies resist assimilation causing tension, conflict, and antagonism of com-peting languages and cultures, which rips nations apart.

2. *Promote multiculturalism and encourage immigrants to maintain their culture.*

Encourage all immigrants to keep their own language and culture. Replace the melting pot metaphor with the salad bowl metaphor.

3. *Celebrate diversity rather than unity.*

Emphasize differences among cultures rather than similarities as Americans, which leaves only tolerance and pluralism to hold us together. Encourage various cultural subgroups living in America

4. *Encourage the least educated to migrate to America.*

Creates an unassimilated, undereducated, and antagonistic underclass to the population.

5. *Invest in ethnic identity.*

Blame all minority failure on those in the majority, which encourages victimology and resentment.

6. *Encourage dual Citizenship.*

Dual citizenship promotes divided loyalties.

7. *Make questioning the cult of diversity taboo.*

Words like 'racist' or 'xenophobe' stop discussion and paralyze questioning.

8. *Don't enforce immigration laws.*

Arnold Toynbee observed that all great civilizations rise and fall. He said, "An autopsy of history would show that all great nations commit suicide." The future of our great nation is deeply in trouble and worsening fast. If we don't get the illegal immigration problem solved quickly, it will rage like a California wildfire to destroy everything in its path, especially The American Dream.

*In the first place we should insist when an immigrant
comes here in good faith he becomes an American,
assimilates himself to us, he shall be treated on an
exact equality with everyone else, for it is an outrage
to discriminate against any such man because of creed,
for birthplace or origin but this is predicated upon this
persons becoming in every facet an American and nothing but an American. There can be no divided allegiance
here. Any man who says he's an American but something
else also isn't an American at all.* We have room but for
one flag, the American Language here and that is the
English language, We have room for one sole loyalty
and that is the loyalty to the American people.

— Teddy Roosevelt

There is an element that seeks to undermine *E pluribus unum.*
It seeks to hyphenate Americans—to develop linguistic division to assign rights and preferences based on race and ethnicity diversity and elevate devotion to foreign ideology and
traditions while at the same time to denigrating American
culture, American values, American founding principles. In
order to do so they know that they have to stop the process of
assimilation and in order to do that they must undermine our
immigration laws.

To preserve America we must insist that new citizens learn
our culture and customs and become Americans—without any
hyphens.

To preserve America
we must insist that new
citizens learn our culture
and customs and become
Americans
—without any hyphens.

Part Five

Freedom Revolution

"Those who expect to reap the blessings of freedom must, like men, undergo the fatigue of supporting it."

— Tom Paine

"The battle, Sir, is not to the strong alone; it is to the vigilant, the active, the brave.

— Patrick Henry

The Pledge of Allegiance

The Pledge of Allegiance was written in August 1892 by the minister Francis Bellamy. It was originally published in *The Youth's Companion*. In its original form it read:

> *I pledge allegiance to my Flag and the Republic for which it stands, one nation, indivisible, with liberty and justice for all.*

In 1923, the words, "the Flag of the United States of America" were added. At that time it read:

> *I pledge allegiance to the Flag of the United States of America and to the Republic for which it stands, one nation, indivisible, with liberty and justice for all.*

In 1954, in response to the Communist threat of the times, President Eisenhower encouraged Congress to add the words "under God," creating the 31-word Pledge of Allegiance of today:

> *I pledge allegiance to the flag of the United States of America and to the republic for which it stands, one nation under God, indivisible, with liberty and justice for all.*

21

Who Determines Constitutionality?

There is fundamental battle for freedom and liberty based on the uniquely American Experiment of Federalism. Federalism is the sharing of power between a federal government and the various state governments, and this foundation is at the very heart of the battle.

In recent years, the federal government has demonstrated that absolute power is its sole desire. They have ignored the message delivered through Tea Parties and have directly engaged in political battles with state governments. If "we the people" lose these battles, *all* power will centralize in Washington D.C. and the dynamics of our free country will rapidly change from a government that serves the people to a government that dictates to the people. The crisis ultimately revolves around this question:

"Who decides the constitutionality of a federal law?"

The most visible battle centers around the unconstitutional health care bill passed in March 2010. But as this one proceeds, there are other Constitutional battles cueing up in the pipeline. Many states where the population embraces freedom have begun to draft legislation that challenges federal authority on matters that the federal government has already overstepped their authority; and, proactive states are preparing legislation in preparation for future offenses. Some examples of these battles:

> The Fed is changing from a government that services the people to a government that dictates to the people.

- Federal Health Care legislation designed to redistribute wealth and make states and people massively dependent on the federal government.

- Federal Cap and Trade legislation designed to foster more state dependence of federal funds by making them insolvent through excessive taxation.

- Federal Amnesty legislation designed to increase the voter base for federal level redistribution schemes.

- Federal Financial Reform legislation designed to acquire more economic power at the federal level to use a coercive tools against states and the people.

- State Firearm Legislation that denies federal authority over firearms produced within a states; this is designed to proactively challenge the federal governments grasp on firearm laws by eliminating the "commerce clause" argument.

Each one of these battles between states and federal governments test the very foundation of federalism upon which our great country has prospered in relative political, economic, and individual freedom. If the pillar of Federalism is to fall, the entire house of cards of the American Experiment will fall with it, and a centralized authority will be formed. Our children's future will be sealed as servants to corrupt politicians in Washington D.C.

Will the Supreme Court Uphold the Constitution?

The first question that must be resolved is "will the Supreme Court uphold the Constitution?" Almost half of the state governments are participating in a lawsuit claiming that the health care bill is unconstitutional. One of the multiple points of contention has to do with the federal governments new power to force a private citizen, under penalty of law, to purchase a product. It is clearly unconstitutional and something that has never been demanded by federal law before.

This is the federal court's chance to clearly reassert the state's constitutionally empowered jurisdiction and put the federal government back under the chains of federalism as defined by the Constitution. If they are willing and able to do this in no uncertain terms, we may still avoid a full Constitutional Crisis. If, on the other hand, the federal court sides with the federal legislators, then they will have missed the golden opportunity to restore stability and liberty to this country and will have placed us on a road to a government of absolute power.

Past rulings indicate that judges are, as Jefferson warned, simply people too; with political ambitions and a willingness to apply arbitrary opinions over rule-of-law. In fact, Supreme Court Justice Sotomayor, appointed by President Obama in 2009, publicly argued the merits of rulings based on social justice over rule-of-law. Can an idea be any more dangerous to liberty than that?

In the 1942 case *Wikard v. Filburn*, the Supreme Court ruled that a farmer growing wheat, on his own property, for his own consumption, is subject to federal laws. The ruling was based on a laughable "commerce clause" interpretation that claimed that since the farmer was *not* participating in interstate commerce then the farmer affected interstate commerce. This kind of circular thinking was used to steal the freedom and liberty from this farmer so that federal power might be increased. It was an impossible step of logic, but rulings like this are used as a precedent for incredible interpretations of the enumerated powers in the Constitution.

What precedent is set if the health care legislation is deemed constitutional and the federal government immediately acquires "constitutional" power to mandate private citizen purchases? No doubt, this precedent will be used to force Americans to purchase all kinds of products that "partner" corporations might offer. What warped definition of "liberty" encompasses this concept?

Who Has the Final Say?

If the Supreme Court rules in favor of the federal government and deems an obviously unconstitutional law to be constitutional then tensions between the states and the federal government will increase significantly. At this point, the Constitutional crisis will expose its head for all to see, and the fundamental question at the heart of it all is:

"Who decides the constitutionality of a federal law?"

The Constitution does not answer this question. The precedent is that the Supreme Court rules on these. But, what happens when "we the people" judge the Supreme Court to be part of the problem?

First, consider that the common idea is that the Supreme Court offers the final say on what is Constitutional. This is partially true given past history and other Supreme Court rulings. But take notice that historically the Supreme Court assumed this power for itself; it was not allocated through the Constitution. This power of final authority was first considered with *Marbury v. Madison* in 1803 and accrued through other cases presided over by Supreme Court Justice Marshal, a well-known champion of centralized federal power. It's easy to see the conflict of interest when a federal judicial branch deems itself to hold absolute authority over the constitutionality of federal laws and federal executive actions. Over time a federal court will become more and more emboldened to ignore the states and "we the people" and rule in favor of more centralized federal power.

The Constitution is silent on this and does not provide the answer. This was intentional, because in all matters "we the people" are the final authority. Giving the federal judicial branch the supreme power of determination institutionalizes an obvious danger to freedom and liberty. This danger was described by Thomas Jefferson.

"....To consider the judges as the ultimate arbiters of all constitutional questions is a very dangerous doctrine indeed, and one which would place us under the despotism of an oligarchy. Our judges are as honest as other men and not more so. They have with others the same passions for party, for power, and the privilege of their corps...and their power is more dangerous as they are in office for life and not responsible, as the other functionaries are, to the elective control. The Constitution has erected no such tribunal, knowing that to whatever hands confided, with the corruption of time and party, its members would become despots...."

—Thomas Jefferson

In 1798, Jefferson and Madison authored the Virginian and Kentucky Resolutions in response to the Alien and Sedition acts. The resolution argued that unconstitutional federal bills that became federal law were null and void and of no effect. According to Jefferson and Madison, states were to be the ultimate arbiter on which laws were constitutional and which were not. By nullifying unconstitutional laws state governments need not ask permission of federal courts to govern their sovereign states.

The Crisis Resolved

What's it going to be? Will we move to freedom through decentralized government in which the people and the states determine the constitutionality of federal laws. With this choice, federalism is restored and sovereign states each govern themselves locally through rule-of-law.

Or, will we move to servitude to a centralized government in which all three federal branches work together to pass laws, enforce laws, and judge their own laws constitutional. With this choice, the Constitution and federalism are destroyed, absolute power is centralized and rule-of-men will dominate law.

This question is ultimately answered by the will of the people. We will decide and it will have immeasurable impact on our country's future.

Authored by Brian Roberts, State Chapter Coordinator for the Texas Tenth Amendment Center. http://www.tenthamendmentcenter.com. Copyright: 2010 by TenthAmendmentCenter.com. Permission to reprint this article in whole or in part is gladly granted provided full credit is given.

Treason From Within

A nation can survive its fools, and even the ambitious. But it cannot survive treason from within. An enemy at the gates is less formidable, for he is known and carries his banner openly. But the traitor moves amongst those within the gate freely, his sly whispers rustling through all the alleys, heard in the very halls of government itself. For the traitor appears not a traitor; he speaks in accents familiar to his victims, and he wears their face and their arguments, he appeals to the baseness that lies deep in the hearts of all men. He rots the soul of a nation, he works secretly and unknown in the night to undermine the pillars of the city, he infects the body politic so that it can no longer resist. A murderer is less to fear.

—Marcus Tullius Cicero

22

The Tenth Amendment

The Constitution grants Congress seventeen specific delegated powers. Commands in the 9th and 10th Amendments state that powers not articulated and thus not delegated by the Constitution to the Congress are reserved to the States and to the people. Congress can only use its delegated powers to legislate for the general welfare—meaning it cannot spend tax dollars on individuals or selected groups, but only for all of us. Congress cannot deny equal protection of the laws—thus it must treat similarly situated entities in a similar manner.

Much of Congress' legislation, such as the bail out of large banks, taking over the automotive industry, mandating that citizen purchase health care runs a foul of Constitutional principles. The people we send to the federal government seem to be unable to legislate within Constitutional limits.

The 10th Amendment defines the total scope of federal power as being that which has been delegated by the people to the federal government, and also that which is absolutely necessary to advancing those powers specifically enumerated in the Constitution of the United States. The rest is to be handled by the State governments, or locally, by the people themselves.

The Constitution does not include any congressional power to override State laws.

The Constitution does not include any congressional power to override State laws. It does not give the judicial branch unlimited jurisdiction over all

matters. It does not provide Congress with the power to legislate over everything. This is verified by the simple fact that
attempts to make these principles part of the Constitution were
soundly rejected by the Founders.

If the Congress had been intended to carry out anything
they claim would promote the "general welfare," what would
be the point of listing its specific powers in Article I, Section 8
since these would already be covered?

The 10th Amendment was adopted after the Constitutional
ratification process to emphasize the fact that the States remained individual and unique sovereignties; that they were
empowered in areas that the Constitution did not delegate to
the federal government. With this in mind, any federal attempt
to legislate beyond the Constitutional limits of Congress'
authority is a usurpation of State sovereignty—and is unconstitutional.

Tragically, the 10th Amendment has been largely ignored,
but there are a great many reasons to bring it to the forefront.
Keep in mind that the Founders envisioned a loose confederation of States—not a one-size-fits-all solution for everything
that could arise. Governments and political leaders are best
held accountable to the will of the people when government is
local. The people of a State know what is best for them; they
do not need bureaucrats thousands of miles away, governing
their lives.

The politicians, especially the progressives, are frustrated
with the Constitution because it places strict limits on the
federal government's actions. They want a "living" constitution—one that changes with the times and politicians' desires.
Our Constitution protects us from the encroachments of government power—a living constitution will not.

Copyright © 2009 by TenthAmendmentCenter.com. Permission to reprint in whole
or in part is gladly granted, provided full credit is given.

23

States Push Back

A merica's Founding Fathers were concerned that the federal government would become tyrannical if it became too powerful. So they put checks and balances on it's power. The Constitution enumerates 17 powers that the federal government may exercise, and forbids any others. One of these was that Washington should be restrained by the powers of the States, which would retain a high degree of sovereignty. The 10th Amendment to the Constitution is explicit:

> *The powers not delegated to the United States by the Constitution, nor prohibited by it to the States, are reserved to the States respectively, or to the people.*

The Founders insisted that States retain their borders, integrity and their sovereignty to be able to resist federal encroachment and to govern themselves—even without the federal government, if necessary. The federal government is also expected to abide by rules—in its case, the Constitution of the United States.

The people we send to the federal government to legislate take an oath to uphold the Constitution, yet they seem to forget their oath and ignore the Constitution. Much of congressional legislation, such as bailing out large banks, runs a foul of Constitution principles.

Increasingly Americans are fed up and disgusted with federal politics. Actions by the federal government—particularly under President Obama—bare an uncanny similarity to the actions by Great Britain just before the America Revolution.

The 10th Amendment Movement

The 10th Amendment Movement is an effort to push back against unconstitutional federal laws and regulations on a State level. It is not a movement by the States to secede from the Union, but rather an attempt to persuade the federal government to abide by the Constitution. The principle is known as "nullification" and was recognized by the Founders as one of the States' potent tools for containing an over-reaching federal government.

Leading the charge was Oklahoma. In 2010, its House of Representatives passed House Joint Resolution 1003 by a vote of 83 to 13, resolving *"that the State of Oklahoma hereby claims sovereignty under the Tenth Amendment to the Constitution of the United States over all powers not otherwise enumerated and granted to the federal government by the Constitution of the United States."*

HJR 1003 also states *"that this serves as Notice and Demand to the federal government, as our agent, to cease and desist, effective immediately, mandates that are beyond the scope of these constitutionally delegated powers."* It directs that copies of the resolution be distributed to, among others, the President of the United States, the president of the U.S. Senate, and the Speaker of the U.S. House of Representatives.

Two months later, South Dakota became the second State in the nation to have both its House and Senate pass 10th Amendment resolutions. Arizona, Hawaii, Montana, Michigan, Missouri, New Hampshire, and Washington soon introduced resolutions declaring State sovereignty under the 9th and 10th Amendments. They seek a rollback of federal authority under the powers enumerated in the Constitution, with the States assuming the governance of the non-enumerated powers, as required by the 10th Amendment.

Some State legislators feared if they support such a resolution, they might face funding cuts from Washington as retribution. But it was precisely through the bait of such handouts that the federal government has secured so much of its unconstitutional authority.

Nullification

Nullification is a legal theory that a State has the right to nullify, or invalidate, any federal law that the State deems unconstitutional. The theory is based on a view that the sovereign States formed the Union, and as creators of the compact they hold final authority regarding the limits of the power of the central government. Under the Compact Theory, the States—not the Supreme Court—are the ultimate interpreters of the extent of the national government's power.

The powers delegated by the proposed Constitution to the federal government are few and defined. Those which are to remain in the State governments are numerous and indefinite.

—James Madison

When a State 'nullifies' a federal law, the State proclaims that the law in question is void and inoperative—or "non-effective"—within the boundaries of that State, and is not a law as far as that State is concerned. People on the forefront at the State level press for the 10th Amendment pull back are trailblazers in mounting resistance to over-reaching federal laws.

Firearms Freedom Act

The model for most of these bills came from Montana's Firearms Freedom Act (FFA) that states that any gun or gun accessory manufactured in Montana that is purchased and remains in Montana, cannot be regulated by the federal government. .

The Montana Firearms Freedom Act, also known as Montana House Bill Number 246, was signed in to law by Governor Brian Schweitzer effective on October 1, 2009. The law exempts firearms made and kept in the State of Montana from United States federal firearms regulations. It also has no requirements for registration, background checks or dealer licensing. It applies to firearms other than machine guns, along with ammunition and accessories such as silencers, provided that these items are manufactured in the State, and do not leave the State.

The Firearms Freedom Act nullifies the authority of the federal government to regulate guns within the borders of the State when none of the guns or related products ever leave the State. The federal government has been very successful in the past in regulating all guns through the "Commerce Clause" of the Constitution. Montana's bone of contention is that the Commerce Clause regulates interstate commerce and has no authority over intrastate commerce.

The reasoning behind this is that federal authority for all such regulation stems from the Constitution's "interstate commerce clause." Something that doesn't leave the State isn't part of interstate commerce.

Other States have followed, including Pennsylvania, Idaho, Utah, Missouri, Tennessee, New Hampshire, Wyoming, Alaska, Alabama, Arizona, Colorado, Florida, Indiana, Minnesota, Ohio, Oklahoma, South Carolina, Texas, Virginia, Washington, and South Dakota.

Real ID Nullification

In 2005, the Congress passed the "Real-ID Act" creating national identification standards. The law set forth certain requirements for State driver's licenses and ID cards to be accepted by the federal government for "official purposes", as defined by the Secretary of Homeland Security. These include presenting State driver's licenses and identification cards

> [N]ullification begins with the axiomatic point that a federal law that violates the Constitution is no law at all.
>
> —Thomas E. Woods
> *Nullification:*
> *How to Resist Federal Tyranny*
> *in the 21st Century*

for boarding commercially operated airline flights and entering federal buildings and nuclear power plants. Each State must agree to share its motor vehicle database with all other States. The database must include, at a minimum, all the data printed on the State drivers'

licenses and ID cards, plus drivers' histories, including motor vehicle violations, suspensions, and points on licenses.

Opponents across the political spectrum resisted Real ID as an invasion of privacy, another unfunded mandate, and as another exercise of federal power not authorized by the Constitution.

New Hampshire's House of Representatives overwhelmingly approved HB 1582 that prohibits the New Hampshire from participating in the national ID card system. By 2007, twenty-five States passed non-binding resolutions opposing the law along with binding legislation that nullified the act within the State borders. Even though Real ID remains on the books, its implementation has been "delayed" numerous times in response to this massive State resistance, rendering it effectively null and void.

Sheriffs First Legislation

A "Sheriffs First" bill would make it a State crime for any federal agent to make an arrest, search, or seizure within the State without first getting the advanced, written permission of the elected County Sheriff of the county in which the event is to take place.

Locally-elected Sheriffs are accountable to the people and are supposed to be the chief law enforcement officer of the county, bar none. This bill puts teeth into the expectation that federal agents must operate with the approval of the County Sheriff, or not at all.

It also gives the local Sheriff tools necessary to protect the rights of the people of his county. There are exceptions in the legislation for "hot pursuit", U.S. customs and border patrol, and dealing with corrupt Sheriffs.

State Regulation of Marijuana

Nothing in the Constitution gives the federal government any authority to override State laws on marijuana. All three branches of the federal government, however, have interpreted the Commerce Clause of the Constitution to authorize them to engage in this prohibited activity, even though there's supposedly no "legal" commerce in the plant. At best, these arguments are dubious; at worst they are an intentional attacks on the Constitution and our liberty.

Because marijuana can easily be transported from place to place it comes under the Commerce Clause, according to the Supreme Court, even without *any* evidence of such transport. According to federal law there is no legitimate commerce in marijuana but still claims to regulates it under the Commerce Clause. The argument is circular and convoluted.

Early in 20th century States were experiencing large influx of Mexican immigrants. In those days marijuana use was predominantly associated with Mexicans. Out of an anti-Mexican bias States passed marijuana laws as early as 1913.

1937 Marihuana Tax Act was passed by the 75th Congress under pressure from a progressive group of big business men like Andrew Mellon and Newspaper mogul William Randolf Hearst in order to destroy the hemp industry. The Act did not itself criminalize the possession or usage of hemp, marijuana, or cannabis, but levied a tax equaling roughly one dollar on anyone who dealt commercially in these plants. The Act superseded State laws and included penalty provisions and elaborate rules of enforcement to which marijuana, cannabis, or hemp handlers were subject. Violation of these procedures could result in a fine of up to $2000 and five years' imprisonment.

The 1937 Marihuana Tax Act (MTA) created a catch-22, wherein one could not pay the required tax because the stamp was never issued. As a result marijuana was effectively prohibited until 1969 when part of the law was thrown out as unconstitutional in a lawsuit brought by Timothy Leary. In 1970, Congress passed the Controlled Substances Act (CSA), which repealed the 1937 Act and classified marijuana as a Schedule 1 substance, along with heroin, methamphetamine, and other highly addictive, dangerous drugs.

Medical Marijuana

The MTA passed over objections of the American Medical Association, which doubted the government's claims about marijuana addiction, violence, and overdosage. Further, because the word "Marihuana" was largely unknown at the time, the medical profession did not realize they were losing cannabis as an available medicine. The CSA defines Schedule 1 as having "high potential for abuse, no accredited medical use, and a lack of accepted safety".

In the 1990s, a movement developed around the medicinal use of marijuana and California was the first State to pass a medical marijuana law — state-wide voter initiative Proposition 215, the Compassionate Use Act of 1996.

Subsequently, thirteen States have passed legal exemptions for patients to use and for the cultivate of marijuana for medical use. California has taken the lead in the nullification of the federal prohibition through the use of medical marijuana legislation. Two California counties — San Bernadino and San Diego — refused to acknowledge medical use of marijuana or to abide with California's medical marijuana law because it conflicts with federal law. They filed a lawsuit that lost at every level of appeal in California. The Supreme Court refused to hear it, which means the Court acknowledged that State laws do not have to mimic federal law.

Recreational Use

Millions of otherwise law-abiding Americans use marijuana in the privacy of their homes without adverse reactions. Compared to alcohol marijuana has fewer problems, but it's use is unlawful—prohibited—which is a limit on our liberty and free choice without basis in the Constitution.

Alaska ruled that use of marijuana in one's home is legal and the federal government has not pursued Alaskans into their homes. Nor has the federal government mounted a legal challenge to California's medical marijuana law. The "tax and regulate" law, which effectively legalizes recreational use among adults, was put on the November 2010 ballot in California.

Health Care Reform

Perhaps the biggest State push back has been against the unpopular Health Care Legislation passed in early 2010. Even before the final vote, South Carolina Attorney General Henry McMaster announced that he and Florida Attorney General Bill McCollum would file a federal lawsuit if the health care reform legislation passed. The ink from President Obama's pen had hardly dried when other States began jumping on board. At the heart of the issue was the federal mandate on citizens, forcing them to buy health insurance.

In the States' view the Health Care Reform Bill overreaches the Commerce Clause and is unconstitutional. Buying insurance is commerce but *not buying is not commerce*. Additionally, the bill expands Medicare to put more unfunded mandates on the backs of the States, which were already straining financially after the 2008 economic meltdown, instead of letting States develop and manage their own programs.

Just days before the bill was approved Virginia passed a bill blocking the federal government from forcing people in Virginia to buy insurance. Because Virginia had a bill on the books, it filed a separate suit in Virginia Federal Court known as the "Rocket Docket". The Virginia bill gives "standing", which allows questioning of Congress.

Minnesota Governor Pawlenty told reporters, "We are a republic and this is a dramatic overreach. It is incumbent upon all of us to rise up and say enough is enough!" When Alaska joined the suite, Alaska Governor Alaska Sean Parnell said, "We must stop making it about health care. This is about liberty."

The law imposes a "minimum essential coverage" on most Americans, with a penalty for those who opt out of that coverage. It was this individual mandate that drove 20 states to file the lawsuit, claiming that "Congress is attempting to regulate and penalize Americans for choosing not to engage in economic activity. If Congress can do this much, there will be virtually no sphere of private decision-making beyond the reach of federal power."

Is It a Tax?

During campaign promoting the healthcare law, President Barack Obama admonently insisted that the penalty for individuals who opt out of receiving health insurance is *not* a tax. During an interview with George Stephanopoulos in Fall 2009, Obama said, "For us to say that you've got to take a responsibility to get health insurance is absolutely not a tax increase." When Stephanopoulos pursued the issue further, asking if the individual mandate penalty could be perceived as a tax, the President replied, "Absolutely not. I reject that notion."

Apparently the government recognized the weakness of that defense, because in a July 2010 court hearing the government asserted that the power to levy taxes is even greater than the power to regulate interstate commerce and that the government therefore elected to call the penalty a tax.

The states involved in the lawsuit are Florida, Alabama, Alaska, Arizona, Colorado, Georgia, Idaho, Indiana, Louisiana, Michigan, Mississippi, Nebraska, Nevada, North Dakota, South Carolina, South Dakota, Pennsylvania, Texas, Utah, and Washington.

Immigration Enforcement

One of the most contentious State push backs began with
Arizona Governor Jan Brewer signing Arizona's controversial
immigration bill—BS 1070—into law in Spring of 2010..

Whereas with other issues the problem has been the federal government over-reaching, with immigration the government failed to secure the border or to enforce the laws on
the books to protect the States and its citizens—the federal
government's primary responsibility.

For years Arizona had battled hordes of illegal immigrants
flooding across the border, bringing kidnapping, drug car-
tels, brutal murders, including several beheadings. Governor
Brewer's many letters to President Obama brought no response.
Finally, Arizona crafted and passed a law mirroring the federal
law that permits law enforcement officers to check citizenship
in prescribed situations.

Passage of SB 1070 was met with praise from Arizonians
and citizen support across the nation and with howls from
radical groups like La Raza (The Race) and the politicians
they support. Before even reading the bill, Obama Team criticized the law, saying that it promoted racial profiling—which
was specifically prohibited in the bill.

After many requests were ignored, Governor Brewer was
finally able to meet with President Obama in what was reported
as a tense meeting where he pressed for comprehensive immigration reform while Brewer insisted that securing the border
was a priority. Obama
promised to get back to
her within two weeks with
a decision on his course of
action. He didn't. Instead,
thinking they were ig-
nored again, Governor
Brewer and Arizonians

> The federal government has
> failed to secure the border
> or to enforce the laws on the
> books to protect the States
> and its citizens—it's primary
> responsibility.

learned from an interview on Ecuadorian TV with Secretary of State Hillary Clinton that the U.S. Department of Justice (DOJ) would be suing Arizona. Many were surprised at what seemed to be unveiled contempt for States' rights.

Indeed, the DOJ filed suit against Arizona and Jan Brewer in her capacity as Governor. The surprise was that the suit was not based upon the potential for racial profiling as had been expected after several high-level officials had criticized the bill, but upon the Supremacy Clause.

The day before the law was to go into effect on July 28, 2010 federal judge Susan Bolton injoined the most controversial parts of law, thereby stopping their implementation when the law went into effect on July 29. Upon receiving the Federal complaint, Brewer wondered on national TV why the government did not pursue Rhode Island, which had been following illegal enforcement procedures similar to those in the Arizona bill and why the government did not pursue sanctuary cities, which were deliberately obstructing enforcement of federal law.

Meanwhile, Arizona and citizens across the nation expressed outrage that the federal government was doing little to enforce the federal immigration laws, leaving American citizens and the municipalities where they live struggle with the problems that result from unchecked illegal immigration—yet sue to prevent States from protecting their citizens. Despite the DOJ action, upwards of 44 States were considering enacting laws similar to Arizona's BS 1070.

Supremacy Clause

The Supremacy Clause is a clause in the Constitution—Article VI, Clause 2—that establishes the Constitution, Federal Statutes, and U.S. treaties as "the supreme law of the land."

This Constitution, and the Laws of the United States which shall be made in Pursuance thereof; and all Trea-

*ties made, or which shall be made, under the Authority
of the United States, shall be the supreme Law of the
Land; and the Judges in every State shall be bound
thereby, any Thing in the Constitution or Laws of any
State to the Contrary notwithstanding.*

The Supremacy Clause established the Constitution as
"the Supreme Law of the Land" both in the Federal courts and
in all of the State courts, mandating that all state judges shall
uphold them, even if there are state laws or state constitutions
that conflict with the powers of the Federal government. Use
of the word "shall" which makes it a necessity, a compulsion.

In *Edgar v. Mite Corporation,* 457 U.S. 624 (1982), the
Supreme Court ruled that *"A state statute is void to the extent
that it actually conflicts with a valid federal statute."* This
means that a State law will be found to violate the supremacy
clause when compliance with both federal and State law is
impossible, or when *"...state law stands as an obstacle to the
accomplishment and execution of the full purposes and objec-
tives of Congress..."*

States Push Back

As will be discussed in the next chapter, States lost much
of their power over Congress with the passage of the 17th
Amendment, which substituted State appointment of Senators
by populous elections. Since its ratification in 1913, States'
powers have continually declined until rich lobbyists and other
special interests seem to have more sway than do State legislatures.

A kind of informal State "revolution" is brewing lead by
States that understand what freedom and self-government are
and what it means to protect that foundation. A good indica-
tor of which State governments will or may participate in the
revolution is to observe which States are proactively resisting
the federal government through their own independent political process. Consider what some of the States are proactively

doing to resist federal encroachment. Consider the very character, nature and mentality of the State government systems currently in place to get a better feel for which State governments will remain Tories and which ones Revolutionaries.

The spirit of revolution is not prevalent in every State, but only some States. It is for this reason that would-be tyrants hate the division of power, the independent and separate sovereignty of States and decentralization. It is for this reason that we the people should love it.

I consider the foundation of the Constitution as laid on this ground that "all powers not delegated to the United States, by the Constitution, nor prohibited by it to the states, are reserved to the states or to the people." To take a single step beyond the boundaries thus specially drawn around the powers of Congress, is to take possession of a boundless field of power no longer susceptible of any definition.

—Thomas Jefferson

The 20-teens may emerge as the decade of the 10th Amendment and the return to States' rights. We can hope. As a new chapter is written States need the help of We the People to reclaim their power—the power guaranteed to States by the Founders in the 10th Amendment.

[The purpose of a written constitution is] to bind up the several branches of government by certain laws, which, when they transgress, their acts shall become nullities; to render unnecessary an appeal to the people, or in other words a rebellion, on every infraction of their rights, on the peril that their acquiescence shall be construed into an intention to surrender those rights.

—Thomas Jefferson

24

The 17th Amendment

S eparation of powers is one of our founding principles.
Originally State legislatures welded much more power
over the Congress than they do today because States appointed
Senators and had the power to quickly recall them, which insured that Congress was responsive to the States. For example,
seven Senators were recalled in 1836 for voting against their
constituents' interests. Over the last century, however, so much
power has flowed from the States to the federal government
that States now have little means to control Congress or the
federal government. The balance of power between States and
the federal government shifted dramatically with the advent of
the 17th Amendment, which authorized the election of Senators
in general.

The Founders fought bitterly against popular elections of
Senators because they did not want to repeat the mistakes of
the Athenian and Roman Democracies that lead to welfare
States. Putting selection of Senators in the hands of State Legislatures was meant to keep Congress accountable.

The House of Representatives was to be the voice of the
people. Representatives are elected proportionally for a two-
year term by popular vote. After two years, the people can
reelect the incumbent or vote for a new Representative.

The Senate was to be the voice of the sovereign States that
make up the federal Union. The Founders designed the checks
and balances so that the Senate was given the critically important function of guardian of federalism. The Senate approves

The Founders wanted the sovereign States to have and maintain a direct voice in the affairs of the federal legislature. House-spending proposals, ratifies treaties with foreign nations, approves to presidential appointments, and confirms nominees to the Supreme Court. Each State legislature elected two Senators each to serve for six years or until recalled and replaced.

This process worked without major problems through the mid-1850s, until the American Civil War, when because of increasing partisanship and strife, many State legislatures failed to elect Senators for prolonged periods.

When deadlocked, which was common, a State went without representation in the Senate. In the first Congress, for example, New York had no Senator for three months. The problem of deadlocked legislatures continued unabated from 1887 until 1913—more than a quarter of a century.

In 1866, a Republican majority Congress passed a law under provision of Article I, Section 4 of the Constitution, to require an open voice vote in the election of Senators. With this law, Republicans hoped to gain insight into the senatorial election process in Southern States. By requiring State legislatures to use an open voice for the senatorial elections, serious corruption was allowed to enter the process.

At the beginning of the 20th Century the "Progressive Movement" demanded popular elections of Senators to eliminate corruption. While popular election of Senators was "more democratic", it is opposite from the ideas of the Founders who wanted the sovereign States to have and maintain a direct voice in the affairs of the federal legislature.

The 17th Amendment

The 17th Amendment established direct election of Senators popular vote. The Amendment superseded Article I, § 3. Clauses 1 and 2 of the Constitution, under which Senators were elected by State legislatures. It also altered the procedure for filling vacancies in the Senate, to be consistent with the method of election. It was ratified and took effect on April 8, 1913.

The Senate of the United States shall be composed of two Senators from each State, elected by the people thereof, for six years; and each Senator shall have one vote. The electors in each State shall have the qualifications requisite for electors of the most numerous branches of the State legislatures.

When vacancies happen in the representation of any State in the Senate, the executive authority of such State shall issue writs of election to fill such vacancies: Provided, That the legislature of any State may empower the executive thereof to make temporary appointments until the people fill the vacancies by election as the legislature may direct.

This amendment shall not be so construed as to affect the election or term of any Senator chosen before it becomes valid as part of the Constitution.

The 17th amendment was championed as a way to prohibit political corruption amongst the State legislators by giving power to the voters to elect Senators.

The Amendment has been blamed, together with the 16th Amendment for generally expanding the authority of the Congress in the 20th century. It has been since 1913, when the 17th Amendment was enacted into law, that the 10th Amendment increasingly began to be ignored.

While the 17th Amendment did eliminate deadlocks, it altered the balance of power. Senators have been elected by the voters in a general election ever since. Through this portal the federal government has gradually expanded its control, while State influence has declined to being little more than that of a lobbyist—and often times lobbyists for deep pockets have more sway than do the States.

The new structure encourages federal deficit spending, inappropriate federal mandates, and federal control over many State institutions. Additionally, the change to electing Senators rather than appointing them creates campaign finance issues. When Senators are appointed by their State legislatures, they don't campaign so have no need for campaign financing.

It would have been unimaginable to the Founders that the States would give away their voice in the Congress by ratifying the 17th Amendment. By ratifying the 17th Amendment, the individual, sovereign States relinquished their voice in the affairs of the federal government because they gave up the ability to recall and replace Senators. If a Senator today fails to represent the interests of his State, the people of the State must wait for six long years to be able to vote the Senator out of office.

Movement to Repeal

The Founding Fathers recognized that power would inevitably triumph over principle. So they structured the government such that exercise of self-interest and other offsetting forces would keep constitutionally guaranteed rights in existence.

That arrangement worked reasonably well for over 200 years among the separated powers of the three federal branches — Congress, the Presidency and the Supreme Court. But it has failed to separate the powers between the once sovereign States and the federal government.

Whoever controls the Senate, controls the government. The Senate approves House spending, ratifies treaties, consents to presidential appointments and confirms Supreme Court appointees, which is guaranteed to continue to concentrate power in the federal government. Conflict between the States and federal government can be expected to get worse.

The most efficient method of regaining constitutional balance is to return to the original constitutional structure. If Senators were again selected by State legislatures, the longevity of Senate careers would be tethered to their vigilant defense of their State's interest—rather than to the interest of Washington forces of influence.

If the 17th Amendment were repealed the State legislatures would again be partners in the federal political process with the ability to decentralize power when appropriate. This structure would allow the flow of power between the States and the federal government to ebb and flow with the needs of the federal republic. State legislatures would again directly influence the selection of federal judges.

The Senate then would take on its original function—the place where the States are represented in the federal government.

Amendment to Repeal

A number of groups and individuals are working towards the repeal of the 17th Amendment, which requires an Amendment to the Constitution. Phoenix Arizona attorney John MacMullin, has drafted the below proposed Amendment to the Constitution, designed to repeal the 17th Amendment.

AN AMENDMENT TO REPEAL THE SEVENTEENTH AMENDMENT AND RELINK THE STATES TO THE FEDERAL POLITICAL PROCESS

SECTION ONE. The Seventeenth Article of Amendment to the Constitution of the United States is hereby repealed.

SECTION TWO. The Senate of the United States shall be composed of two Senators from each State, selected by the legislature of each State. Each Senator shall serve a six-year term and may be reappointed. Each Senator shall have one vote.

SECTION THREE. Among the duties of each Senator is the primary duty to represent the government of their State, and in particular, their State's Legislature, in the Senate. For the purpose of maintaining communications with its Senators, each State Legislature shall establish a liaison committee and shall specify the duties, procedures, and method of appointment of that committee. This committee shall work with its United States Senators in evaluating the impact of federal legislation on their State. All legislation proposed by Congress, and all treaties proposed, shall be submitted to each State's liaison committee.

SECTION FOUR. Senators are subject to removal by the State Legislature. Removal of a Senator requires a majority of each House of the State Legislature.

SECTION FIVE. Congress is precluded from enacting any legislation affecting the senatorial selection process. Each State Legislature shall enact rules and procedures, consistent with this amendment, related to the selection and removal of Senators.

SECTION SIX. This amendment shall not be so construed as to affect the term of any Senator chosen before it becomes valid as part of the Constitution. The electors in each State shall have the qualifications requisite for electors of the most numerous branches of the State Legislatures.

(john.macmullin@cox.net) practices law in Phoenix, Arizona. He has written extensively in the law literature on the 17th Amendment. See MacMullin J., "Amplifying the Tenth Amendment," 31 Ariz.L.R. 915 (1989) You can receive the Mises Daily Article in your in-box. Go here to subscribe or unsubscribe.

Avenues to Repeal

To amend the Constitution, the Amendment must first be officially proposed by one of two methods. The first method is that the Constitutional Amendment is proposed by 2/3 of the members of each of the Houses of the Congress and then sent

on to the States for approval. Once 2/3 of the States approve
the proposed Amendment, it then takes 3/4 of the States to
ratify the amendment within 7 years.

The second method is that 2/3 of the States make application to the Congress to call a convention of State delegates
for the purpose of proposing a Constitutional Amendment.
The Convention then sets its own rules for proposing the
Amendment. Once the convention of State delegates has
proposed the Amendment, it goes to the States for ratification.
The Amendment must then be ratified within 7 years by 3/4 of
the States.

Returns Power to States

What would happen if an Amendment to repeal the 17th
Amendment were to be ratified? The State legislators within
the sovereign States would again elect their Senators, subject
to their recall and replacement at a moment's notice. The election this time will constitutionally specify a "secret ballot".
The people elected to serve in the Senate will then again argue
with passion for the interests of their State instead simply
promoting the interests of their campaign money donors. The
level and quality of oratory will markedly improve as legislation now has to be passed by arguing the merits to convince
10,000 legislators at home. The diversity of opinion and
solutions proposed by the Senate then would truly reflect the
diversity among the fifty States.

Only by changing the architecture of power will we change
the shape and exercise of power. Senators still would be just as
likely to be corrupted. But the corruption would be dispersed
to the 50 separate State legislatures. The corruption more often
would be on behalf of State interests. And its remedy would be
achievable by the vigilance of voters for more responsive State
legislative seats—typically, about less than 50,000 residences
per State legislator, rather than Senate seats—the entire population of the State, usually millions.

Repeal of the 17th Amendment is not in the interest of large corporations, such as banks, large manufacturing companies, labor unions, media, foundations, universities. All of which have interest in legislation emanating from the Congress. Regardless of which political party is in power, the ratification of the 17th Amendment made cost effective the lobbying effort in Washington, D.C. engaged in by these large organizations. The repeal of the 17th Amendment would jeopardize the influence these large organizations have on federal legislation.

If the American people want a chance to save the Republic, the repeal of the 17th Amendment will take us to that goal. It is only the people of the individual, sovereign States who can accomplish this. No one else can, no court, no proclamation, no executive order, only the people. Yet, the people have little awareness and understanding of the issue, which gives power to the special interests who can be counted on to act in their own best interest and not that of the people or the nation.

I see,... and with the deepest affliction, the rapid strides with which the federal branch of our government is advancing towards the usurpation of all the rights reserved to the States, and the consolidation in itself of all powers, foreign and domestic; and that, too, by constructions which, if legitimate, leave no limits to their power... It is but too evident that the three ruling branches of [the Federal government] are in combination to strip their colleagues, the State authorities, of the powers reserved by them, and to exercise themselves all functions foreign and domestic.

—Thomas Jefferson

25

Bring God Back

Y ou don't have to be a religious churchgoer or a devotee to any creed to be concerned about the increasing suppression of God in the marketplace, in the public square, in our schools—in our lives. We need to bring God back. Here's why.

It has been accept as "fact" that the Founding Fathers wanted a separation of church and state. This erroneous notion has been employed to separate us from our divine nature, banishing the spiritual from our lives. Some credit ACLU attorney Leo Pfeffer with the establishment of separation of church and state in the 1947 Supreme Court case *Everson v. Board of Education of Ewing Township*.

The phrase "separation of church and state" is not in any of the founding documents. It is a phrased plucked out of a letter from Thomas Jefferson to the Danbury Baptists. Jefferson's original meaning was that the church was to be protected from the government, not the reverse, which is the case today.

In God We Trust

It is revisionist history to say that God or spirituality was not involved in the founding of American. The Founding Fathers were devotedly religious, some even had seminary degrees. They knew the importance of faith in the Divine. The Founding Fathers regularly prayed. They prayed in church. They prayed before and after meals. They prayed at public meeting and at political meetings.

The Continental Congress of 1782 under the presidency of John Hansen gave money for the printing and distribution of a Bible produced by Mr. Robert Aitken, knows as *The Bible of the Revolution*, which was the first English Bible printed in America. Spiritual symbols and "In God we trust" appear on our money.

There is a heated debate whether the Founders were Christians or Deists. It is an interesting debate for a another discussion. The point here is the Founders pointed to a "Creator" from which unalienable Rights were endowed upon all people — as compared to an all powerful State that grants rights as it sees fit and as is practical for it — the All-Powerful State.

Banishing God

There are frequent lawsuits in which one single atheist takes offense to a religious symbol — usually Christian — demanding that it be removed. It matters not that it may represent decades of tradition or is wanted by tens of thousands of Americans. One atheist, along with a few ACLU attorneys, can force the rest of us to bow to one person's sensibilities. The dispute over the Mount Soledad Cross in La Jolla, California is an example. In 1954, the Mount Soledad Cross replaced an older cross that had been erected in 1913 on the site — a public park maintained by tax dollars.

Some said it is an Easter Cross; others insisted it was a War Memorial. There was continuous litigation since 1989 attempting to remove the cross. Phillip Paulson, who filed the first suit against the City of San Diego, was "offended" by what he saw as a Christian symbol on public land, which his attorneys claimed violated the "no preference" clause of the Constitution. Judges ruled in the favor of the plaintiff, who died sometime ago, a number of times. The taxpaying citizens paying for the cross wanted to keep it. No matter, the *one* deceased atheist was offended. So the cross had to go! The struggle continued until vandals ripped the cross down in 2010.

Numerous judges, government bureaucrats and employers have forbidden employees, and teachers and county clerks from wishing folks "Merry Christmas", banished Christmas trees, which must be called "Holiday trees" and demanded that *Silent Night* be called "Winter Night". Yet, curiously everyone—especially our government—seems to be falling all over themselves to accommodate Muslin's worship of Islam, including feet washing stations, exemptions in prisons so muslins can have face hair, as examples. So while we all must be extraordinarily "sensitive" to Muslin's religious symbols and practices, those of Christians are maligned and banished. This in and of itself is curious—and worrisome.

In 2010, an activist Federal Judge Crabb in Wisconsin outlawed the National Day of Prayer as unconstitutional. The National Day of Prayer was signed into law by Harry Truman in 1952 and in the 1980s Ronald Reagan designated the first Thursday in May to the National Day of Prayer Day. One can pray to any god they choose with a prayer from any religion they support—so no particular religion was being supported by the State. No, the judge ruled that the activity of praying itself, if encouraged by the State, is unconstitutional

Free Exercise of Religion

The 1st Amendment says *"Congress shall make no law restricting the establishment of religion, or prohibiting the free exercise thereof...."* It would seem that outlawing the National Day of Prayer is "prohibiting free exercise" of one's right to pray, but apparently not according to Judge Crabb. While

Judges like Crabb say they are protecting us from religious suppression, the result of their rulings is suppressive—especially of Christian rituals and symbols—to stamp out religion and make the State the god that gives—and takes away—rights.

> You don't need God anymore, you have us Democrats.
>
> —Nancy Pelosi
> Speaker of the House
> Quoted 2006

This is a dangerous trend. All totalitarian regimes get rid of God in the course of their takeover of the people. God holds despots back. When the State grants us our rights, the State can take them back—including the "right to life"!!!! When we are endowed with unalienable rights from our Creator, we are divine beings who may not be aborted, murdered or abused by the State. An 85-year-old senior who doesn't work, is still a divine being entitled to good health care, for example. By contrast, if the State gives us the right to health care, the State can reduce it or take it away. The State can decide that the non-working 85-year-old senior is not useful enough to warrant the collective paying for his or her care. Similarly, when ultrasound reveals that an unborn child has Downs Syndrome, that child is still a divine being endowed by his or her Creator with the right to life under our Constitution—under traditional American values. By contrast, when rights are endowed by the State, the State can decide that such a handicapped infant is a drain on the collective and order the baby aborted—even against the will of the mother!

Role of the Divine

That our rights are endowed upon us by our Creator is what makes our founding so unique. The Declaration of Independence proclaimed: *"We hold these truths to be self-evident, that all men are created equal, that they are all endowed by their Creator with certain unalienable Rights that among these are Life, Liberty, and the pursuit of Happiness."* Some historians maintain that these are the most significant words in American history. Our American Creed is rooted in this Declaration.

We must hold to this—that our rights are endowed by our Creator—written in capital "C". The Founders chose each word with considerable care for particular meanings. Notice that the Declaration states "endowed by their Creator". It doesn't say "the" Creator or "a" Creator, which implies one particular Creator for all. It says "their" Creator, suggesting we each may have different Creators—but all are divine. That our Rights—to live, to be free and to pursue what we choose—are granted by the Divine—whatever that means to each individual—and not by the State.

State Granted Rights

Why is this so significant? Authoritarian States grant citizens their rights. The State is all-powerful and the State can take what it has given. The 1977 USSR Constitution, for example, had 30 Articles describing the Rights that the State granted the People, including right to work, right to rest and leisure, to health protection, maintenance in old age, to housing, to education.

This all sounds fantastic—at first. But who decides which home you get? Which school you attend? Do you think your son or daughter will get to go to Harvard, as President Obama did? Who decides which job is assigned to you? What career you will pursue? The State makes these decisions, not you.

Hold to the Constitution

Our Constitution is unique in two ways. First, it is based on values, rather than demographics. Secondly, *it restrains the government*. The Constitution enumerates certain powers to the central government. Any power not specifically granted to the government, stays with the people and the State. Most Constitutions, such as that for the USSR, describe what the central government will *do for* citizens. A leading progressive, Woodrow Wilson, President from 1902 to 1910, viewed the Constitution as "pre-modern and cumbersome" and pressed to replace it with a parliamentary system. In 1944, FDR proposed a "Second Bill of Rights" to be implemented politically, but not through the Courts. Roosevelt maintained that the "political rights" guaranteed by the Constitution and the Bill of Rights had "proved inadequate to assure us equality in the pursuit of happiness". He proposed creating an "economic bill of rights" which would guarantee a job with a living wage, freedom from unfair competition and monopolies, a home, medical care, education, and recreation. FDR's Second Bill of Rights is very similar to the Rights guaranteed by the Soviet State.

Even more worrisome is President Obama's view that the Constitution is flawed. In a 2001 radio station interview he said:

> ...the Supreme Court never ventured into the issues of redistribution of wealth, and of more basic issues such as political and economic justice in society. To that extent, as radical as I think people try to characterize the Warren Court, it wasn't that radical. **It didn't break free from the essential constraints that were placed by the Founding Fathers in the Constitution,** at least as it's been interpreted, and the Warren Court interpreted in the same way, that generally the Constitution is a charter of negative liberties. Says what the states can't do to you. Says what the federal government can't do to you, but doesn't say what the federal government or state government must do on your behalf. (Emphasis mine)

The Constitution protects us from a tyrannical government. President Obama, just like FDR and Wilson before him wants to remove the constraints placed in the Constitution by our Founding Fathers. These progressive presidents want a Constitution that says what the State will do for Americans, rather than how it will restrain government to protect our unalienable rights. Redistribution of wealth—our wealth, but not his—is a priority for Obama and he laments that the Courts have thus far failed to "break free from the essential constraints" in the Constitution. Life, liberty and the pursuit of happiness as the Declaration speaks are opportunities, not guarantees.

Unalienable Rights

What the State gives, the State can take back. When we are no longer endowed by our Creator—a divine power—we become like cattle. The State looks upon its large population in terms of numbers, statistic and actuarial tables. The State may determine, for example, that there are not enough resources to support older people and ration what is available—or reallocate it to another group, such as 40-year-olds who contribute more.

There was an outcry from feminists in 2010 when a government panel determined that only women over 50-years old would be reimbursed for mammograms. Previously the American Cancer Society advised that women begin screening at 40. In terms of population management, yes, a percentage of women will contract cancer in their forties—but it is a small and acceptable percentage—unless it is you or your mother or sister or wife or daughter. The State can give the right of life and health care and the State can take it away with rationing and "death panels". But the State cannot take away rights endowed by our Creator—the divine. This is why I want God back.

Actuarial Tables

To the State, we large groups of citizens must be managed. Like insurance companies, governments use actuarial tables to determine our predicted life expectancy. So you are healthier and more vigorous than your age-peers? No matter, government looks at statistics and this will determine the level of health care to which the State says *you* are entitled—and the State will not permit you to use your own money to buy the care you seek.

Similarly, there is debate as to when a human becomes "human". Is it at conception? Is it when the fetus looks hu-

Killing The Unfit

The moment we face it frankly we are driven to the conclusion that the community has a right to put a price on the right to live in it ... If people are fit to live, let them live under decent human conditions. If they are not fit to live, kill them in a decent human way. Is it any wonder that some of us are driven to prescribe the lethal chamber as the solution for the hard cases which are at present made the excuse for dragging all the other cases down to their level, and the only solution that will create a sense of full social responsibility in modern populations?

—George Bernard Shaw
Prefaces

man-like? When it kicks? Is it at the first breath in the moment of birth? White House Czar Zeke Emanuel speculates that we become "human" much later when the infant develops a sense of "self" around two years old. The State has already legalized "partial birth abortions" where the baby is aborted—ah, killed?—as it comes out the birth canal. This is actually "legal". Suppose a government panel determines we're not human until, say, two years old, then will the State legalize "post birth" abortions of special needs babies.

When the grantor of our rights changes from our Creator to the State, eugenics becomes a threat. We are not divine beings—just a mass of humanity, like a herd of cattle. Just like a rancher will "thin out" a herd by killing off the weak and sickly ones, so, too, will the State. A special needs child is not divine and too costly—imperfect. Resources should go to the smarter and better looking children.

By comparison when humans are endowed with a Right to Life by the divine, then old people are entitled to live, even when they no longer work. A special needs child is a child of God and has a right to live and to a decent quality of life. A person of a disfavored race has a right to live.

It is this distinction that renders the Obamacare Bill so important—historic. With the passing of the bill the State granted the people a *right*—a right to health care. Hereafter, the federal government can decide to what level of care you and I are entitled. Or perhaps, we will get counseling and a pain pill that Obama suggested was appropriate for grandma needing a hip replacement. Yes, you have a right to health care, but you do not have a right to more than you deserve and the State will determine what *you* deserve by your value to the "collective'.

Eugenics is the practice of selective breeding selective of humans including extermination of "undesired" population groups, with the aim of improving the species. Eugenics was widely popular in the early decades of the 20th century, but fell into disrepute after becoming associated with Nazi Germany.

Agenda 21

You probably don't believe that the State would actually take actions that would lead to you or your loved ones dying sooner than you would otherwise die or actions to actually cause its citizens to die. Yes, you've heard of Mao who murdered some 50-80 million Chinese, Hitler who put 3 million Jews into ovens, and other despots who murdered—but it seems so remote and in the distant past. Surely, no civilized people would permit themselves to be cowed like this—definitely not here in America.

Take a look at Agenda 21 and think again. Agenda 21 is a United Nations Environment Program (UNEP). It is a comprehensive blueprint of action adopted in June 1992 by 178 governments to be taken globally, nationally and locally by organizations of the UN, governments, and major groups in every area in which humans directly affect the environment. The Program for Further Implementation of Agenda 21 was strongly reaffirmed at the World Summit on Sustainable Development (WSSD) held in Johannesburg, South Africa in 2002. It includes combating poverty, changing consumption patterns, population and demographic dynamics, promoting health, promoting sustainable settlement patterns and integrating environment and development into decision-making, atmospheric protection, atmospheric combating deforestation, protecting fragile environments, biodiversity, and pollution control. Sounds great, right? Wrong!

According to supporters, this ambitious agenda will be achieved by concentrating humans in a few small areas of the world and by returning human life to that of a peasant farmer in earlier centuries. Most importantly Agenda 21 calls for cutting world the population by 70-90%. Baring a pandemic where most people die, or unleashing weapon of mass destruction, participating governments—and the USA government is very supportive of Agenda 21—will have to use eugenics to dramatically reduce the birth rate as well as to quicken folks to the great beyond.

Agenda 21 has endowed Rights upon nature. Trees have rights; wolves have rights; rivers have rights, rocks have rights. And these rights supercede those of humans! This is what happens when the State becomes God. In pursuit of protecting the rights of trees, wolves, rivers and rocks, Agenda 21 has mapped the world and where humans will be permitted to live and work, and where we may visit. Most of earth will be totally off limits to human. If you live in one of these restricted areas, which are massive, you will be moved. It is quite startling what governments can do when we give them power and they replace God as endower of our Rights.

26

We the People Push Back

The Constitution was designed by the Founders to restrain government because they knew-well that governments seek to govern and in the process they acquire more and more power. As government grows, individual liberty shrinks. In drafting the Constitution, the Founders put preservation of individual liberty upper most but disagreed as to how to protect it. Anti-Federalists pressed for the enumeration of specific rights because the Constitution conferred so much power on the federal government, while the Federalists were concerned that a Constitutional enumeration of specific liberties could imply that other rights would be surrendered to the government.

They compromised by adding ten Amendments, which they called The Bill of Rights. The 9th Amendment was included specifically to address the Federalists' worry about the federal government assuming anything not specifically addressed.

The 9th Amendment

The enumeration in the Constitution, of certain rights, shall not be construed to deny or disparage others retained by the people.

The 9th Amendment states that there are certain rights listed in the Constitution, but that does not mean that there aren't other rights reserved for the people have that are not enumerated. *The individual has a presumption of liberty.* There are latent rights still to be evoked and enacted into law. The 9th Amendment has rarely been used, to date, it seems no one has been able to unlock its protections and treasures. So far it has only been called upon in adjunct briefs and never as the primary thrust.

There have been very few court cases to flush out 9th Amendment protections. In *Griswold v. Connecticut*, 381 U.S. 479 (1965), a Connecticut law that prohibited the use of contraceptives was successfully challenged when the Supreme Court ruled that the Constitution protects an individual's right to privacy by a vote of 7-2. Justice Arthur Goldberg wrote a concurring opinion in which he used the 9th Amendment to defend the ruling.

Gonzales v. Raich (previously *Ashcroft v. Raich*), 545 U.S. 1 (2005) is another case that endeavored to call on the 9th Amendment. Early in the 2000s two California women, who had been treating their severe chronic pain with homegrown marijuana, filed suit after the plants were destroyed by federal agents. Under California law growing and using marijuana for medical purposes is legal, but illegal under federal law. Angel Raich of Oakland, California who suffered from a brain tumor, Diane Monson of Oroville, California, who suffered from degenerative spinal disease and two anonymous caregivers sued for injunctive and declaratory relief to stop the government from interfering with their right to produce and use medical marijuana claiming that the Controlled Substances Act, which criminalizes cultivation, possession and use of marijuana violates the Commerce Clause, the Due Process Clause of the 5th Amendment, the 9th Amendment, the 10th Amendment, and the doctrine of medical necessity.

The Cato Institute, Institute for Justice, NORML, along with several libertarian organizations and groups opposing the War on Drugs filed briefs for Raich and Monson. California, Maryland, and Washington along with the attorney generals of the anti-drugs states of Alabama, Louisiana and Mississippi filed a brief supporting Raich on the grounds of state's rights.

The case failed in a vote of 6 to 3, confirming that Congress may ban homegrown cannabis even where states approve its use for medicinal purposes. The majority claimed, among other things, that even small amounts of homegrown pot used solely for medical purposes, under the terms of California's medical marijuana law, could make it impossible for federal law enforcement agencies to police illegal drugs.

The dissent by Chief Justice William Rehnquist, Justice Clarence Thomas, and Justice Sandra Day O'Connor noted that the government "has not overcome empirical doubt that the number of Californians engaged in personal cultivation, possession, and use of medical marijuana, or the amount of marijuana they produce, is enough to threaten the federal regime."

> If Congress can regulate [medical marijuana] under the Commerce Clause, then it can regulate virtually anything—and the Federal Government is no longer one of limited and enumerated powers.
>
> —Justice Clarence Thomas

The 9th Amendment purports to protect the people's right but continues to be an enigma. How can its powers be engaged to protect our individual liberties as the Founders intended? Hopefully, future defenses of the people's rights will find ways to unlock the protections of the 9th Amendment.

Health Care Bill Class Action Challenge

Missouri Lt. Governor Peter Kinder filed a class action challenge of the Health Case Bill in July 2010, asserting that it was unconstitutional "as applied", whereas the suits brought by the States challenged the Constitutionality of the law "on its face". Here the assertion was that when actually applied the bill violated Constitutional rights of the citizens of Missouri.

Each of the plaintiffs in the lawsuit targeted a specific aspect of federal healthcare. One plaintiff whose son suffered from Autism claimed that the federal law imposed a penalty on Missouri, because the legislature required insurance companies cover Autism while the federal law did not. Another plaintiff was a senior citizen who sued because federal law ended her eligibility for Medicare Advantage while allowing some individuals in Florida to stay enrolled in the program. A third plaintiff was a younger single woman who sued because she wanted to purchase inexpensive catastrophic coverage only but was required to purchase more expensive full insurance coverage, which she didn't need and wouldn't use.

Lt. Governor Kinder said each plaintiff claimed a violation of the equal protection clause of the Constitution because federal health care carved out special deals for certain states, triggering unequal treatment of Americans. He said, "I'm out to vindicate important rights that all Missourians have and that they're losing under this law.

Census Resistance

The Founders of our fledgling nation had a bold and ambitious plan to empower the people over their new government. The plan was to count every person living in the newly created United States of America, and to use that count to determine representation in the Congress.

The genius of the Founders was taking a tool of government and making it a tool of political empowerment for the governed over their government. To meet this requirement a national census of the population is conducted every ten year and the data gathered is used to allocate Congressional seats, Congressional apportionment, electoral votes, and government program funding.

Generally Americans have considered the census as rather benign but in 2010 mistrust of the federal government had grown to the point where large numbers of Americans we fear-

The invasive nature of the current census raises questions about how and why government will use the collected information. It also demonstrates how the federal bureaucracy consistently encourages citizens to think of themselves in terms of groups rather than as individual Americans.

—Ron Paul
Texas Congressman

ful of the census process. Rumors flew about the numerous questions on the census form and how that information might be used. Across the nation law-abiding citizens refused to complete the forms or to speak to census workers.

Many insisted that census workers could only legally ask about the number of people in each residence. But this is incorrect. On numerous occasions, the courts have said the Constitution gives Congress the authority to collect statistics in the census. *Morales v. Daley*, 116 F. Supp. 2d 801, 820 (S.D. Tex. 2000) concluded that there was no basis for holding Census 2000 unconstitutional because it did not violate rights to privacy or any other Constitutional provisions.

Where, exactly, is the line? The government explained on the Census Bureau website:

The first censuses in 1790 and 1800 were "simple" counts of population that fulfilled the U.S. Constitution's requirement. While later enumerations met this constitutional mandate, they also gathered greater detail about the nation's inhabitants. As a result, the census has grown from a 'head count' to a tool enabling us to better understand the nation's inhabitants, their pursuits and activities, and needs.

Many Americans have taken this expansion of the census data gathering as government over-reaching. There were loud calls for "civil disobedience" advising people to answer only the question of how many people reside in the dwelling. Census worker encountered widespread resistance—especially to face-to-face interviews in their homes by census workers after completing and returning the official form.

The Minutemen

The Minuteman Project, co-founded by Jim Gilchrist, is an activist organization started in April 2005 by a group of private individuals to monitor the United States-Mexican border's flow of illegal immigration. The name derives from the Minutemen militiamen who fought in the American Revolution. It is a spontaneous grassroots unincorporated gathering of American men and women concerned with illegal immigration and its devastating effects upon our way of life, our culture and National sovereignty.

Tea Party Protests

In 2009 huge numbers of average Americans became increasingly concerned by the steady degradation of freedom after freedom by a seemingly calculated effort to concentrate power in Washington. Sometimes calling them "the sleeping giant", Americans who had never before participated in any protest began standing up and speaking out under a banner called, "Tea Parties".

There's debate as to the catalyst that sparked the Tea Party Protest's seemingly spontaneous appearance. Some credit CNBC Business News editor Rick Santelli who sarcastically criticized the government's plan for refinancing mortgages as promoting bad behavior and called for a "tea party" for traders to gather and dump the derivatives in the Chicago River". By Tax Day 2009, middle Americans had begun protesting massive, irresponsible government spending at Tea Party protests across the nation.

These concerned Americans were widely maligned. House Speaker Nancy Pelosi accused the Tea Parties of being "Astroturf" funded by rich Republicans. They were met with criti-

cisms and accusations of hatred and violence from the mainstream media—even though no one could point to any actual
incidence. When Pelosi, carrying her giant gavel, marched
with her troop, which included several Black Congressmen,
through a Tea Party protesting Obamacare, Tea Partiers were
accused of using the "N-word" and spiting on them—the
media went wild in it condemnation. Andrew Brietbart of Big-
Government.com posted a one hundred thousand dollar reward
for anyone providing video or audio recording of the incident,
but no one ever claimed the money, even though the incident
was widely covered in the mainstream media. Nonetheless, the
media and pundits continued to refer to the incident as a verified "fact" to prove that Tea Party Americans are hate-filled
racists protesting solely because they don't want a Black president. In the summer of 2010 the NAACP released an official
resolution accusing Tea Parties of being racist.

However, despite attempts to discredit and marginalize
them, the Tea Party showed growing power to influence elections and policy.

28th Amendment Movement

Enraged by Congress' wild spending and personal excesses,
We the People began looking for ways to reign in our Representatives and Senators. A ground swell of support grew up
around the possibility of passing a 28th Amendment.

Proposed 28th Amendment

*Congress shall make no law that applies to any citizen
of the United States that does not apply equally to all
US Senators and Representatives. Congress shall make
no law that applies to any US Senator or Representative
that does not apply equally to all citizens of the United
States. All existing laws and regulations that do not meet
these criteria shall be declared null and void!*

There are two procedures for amending the Constitution. The method that has been employed with every Amendment that has been proposed or enacted to date requires that the proposed Amendment be approved by both the Senate and the House of Representatives by a two-thirds majority in each, and then ratified by three-fourths of the states. Considering that the objective of the 28th Amendment is to place restrictions on the very people who must approved it, it is probably unlikely to be approved.

The second method that allows for the Constitution to be amended by the actions of states alone without the approval or any Congressional vote. However, this second method has never been used. Two-thirds of States legislatures must the Constitutional Convention where the Amendments would be proposed.

We the People's Power Grows

Traditionally, there have been few options when a population has become disenchanted with its government. Citizens can "vote the bums out" but these days politicians use donations from special interest to get reelected over the will of their constituency. The people can go to the streets and protest. And we saw that with the Tea Parties. Instead of considering the Tea Partiers call for redress, leaders in the Congress berated, maligned—and ignored—them. As frustration and anger grows little recourse is left for the people but to revolt. Fortunately, today We the People have the internet, which has given Patriots tremendous power in being able to rapidly disseminate information outside of the mainstream media as well as to find others of like thinking. Hopefully, activist attorneys will step up to represent We the People's quest to preserve individual liberty and will unlock the powers of the 9th Amendment.

27

Tea Party Patriots

The colonists of the British Thirteen United Colonies, who rebelled against British control during the American Revolution, called themselves Patriots. Also called Americans, Whigs, Revolutionaries, Congress-Men or Rebels, in July 1776, they declared the United States of America to be an independent nation based on the political philosophy of republicanism, as expressed by pamphleteers Thomas Jefferson, Alexander Hamilton, and Thomas Paine. The most prominent leaders of the Patriots are referred to today by Americans as the Founding Fathers of the United States.

As a group, Patriots comprised men and women representing the full array of social, economic, ethnic and racial backgrounds, including college students like Alexander Hamilton, planters like Thomas Jefferson, merchants like Alexander McDougall, and plain farmers like Daniel Shays and Joseph Plumb Martin.

Colonists who remained loyal to the British Crown called themselves Loyalists or "Tories" or "King's men." Additionally there were many people who remained neutral or said nothing because they did not want to lose trade ties with the British.

No Taxation Without Representation

"No taxation without representation" began as a slogan in 1763–1776 that summarized a primary grievance of the British colonists in the Thirteen Colonies. Many in those colonies believed the lack of direct representation in the distant British Parliament was an illegal denial of their rights as Englishmen, and therefore laws taxing the colonists were unconstitutional.

Patriots believed that the assemblies should control issues relating just to the colonies, which they should be able to run themselves. In fact, they had been running themselves after the period of "salutary neglect" before the French and Indian War. Some radical Patriots tarred and feathered tax collectors and customs officers, making those positions dangerous, especially in New England, where the most Patriots were to be found.

Tea Party

The Tea Party movement is an American populist movement that emerged in 2009 through a series of locally and national protests of several federal laws: the Emergency Economic Stabilization Act of 2008—the bailout, the American Recovery and Reinvestment Act of 2009—the stimulus package, and the Health Care Reform Bills—ObamaCare.

The name "Tea Party" harkens back to the Boston Tea Party of 1773. Tea Party protesters use themes, images and slogans similar to those used during the pre-revolutionary period in American history to dramatize the similarities between those times and these—and to stir patriotic pride in the founding of our great nation.

Tea Party Patriots believe in fiscal responsibility, Constitutionally limited government, and free markets. The loosely

affiliated group reveres the Declaration of Independence, the Constitution and the Bill Of Rights as explained in the *Federalist Papers.*

The First Tea Party in 1773

As a key event in the growth of the American Revolution, the Boston Tea Party was a direct action by colonists in Boston, a town in the British colony of Massachusetts, against the British government. On December 16, 1773, after officials in Boston refused to return three ship loads of taxed tea to Britain, a group of colonists boarded the ships and destroyed the tea by throwing it into Boston Harbor. The incident remains an iconic event of American history, and other political protests often refer to it.

The Tea Party was the culmination of a resistance movement throughout British America against the Tea Act, which had been passed by the British Parliament in 1773. Colonists objected to the Tea Act for a variety of reasons, especially because they believed that it violated their right to be taxed only by their own elected representatives. Protesters had successfully prevented the unloading of taxed tea in three other colonies, but in Boston, embattled Royal Governor Thomas Hutchinson refused to allow the tea to be returned to Britain. He apparently did not expect that the protesters would choose to destroy the tea rather than concede the authority of a legislature in which they were not directly represented.

Contract From America

The Contract from America is a political agenda of the Tea Party movement proposed on April 15, 2010 at the Washington Monument in Washington D.C. It was inspired by former Speaker of the House, Newt Gingrich's 1994 Contract with America, which helped to sweep the Republican into office that year. The project was headed by Ryan Hecker, a 29-year old lawyer from Houston, Texas, and was produced through an online voting process. The percentage of the vote, which each agenda item received, appears in parentheses.

The Contract from America is the Tea Party activists' "legislative blueprint for 2010 and beyond"—a document of ten principles and priorities outlining the movement's agenda for the road ahead.

We, the citizens of the United States of America, call upon those seeking to represent us in public office to sign the Contract from America and by doing so commit to support each of its agenda items and advocate on behalf of individual liberty, limited government, and economic freedom. It lists 10 agenda items that were selected by an online vote of over 450,000 people on Tax Day.

1. **Protect the Constitution**

   Identify constitutionality of every new law: Require each bill to identify the specific provision of the Constitution that gives Congress the power to do what the bill does. (82.03%)

2. *Reject Cap & Trade*

   Reject emissions trading: Stop the "cap and trade" administrative approach used to control pollution by providing economic incentives for achieving reductions in the emissions of pollutants. (72.20%).

3. *Demand a Balanced Budget*

   Demand a balanced federal budget: Begin the Constitutional amendment process to require a balanced budget with a two-thirds majority needed for any tax modification. (69.69%)

4. *Enact Fundamental Tax Reform*

   Simplify the tax system: Adopt a single-rate tax system; eliminate the internal revenue code and replace it with one that is no longer than 4,543 words. (64.90%).

5. *Restore Fiscal Responsibility & Constitutionally Limited Government*

Audit federal government for constitutionality: Create a Blue Ribbon task force that engages in an audit of federal agencies and programs, assessing their Constitutionality, and identifying duplication, waste, ineffectiveness, and agencies and programs better left for the states or local authorities. (63.37%)

6. *End Runaway Government Spending*

Limit annual growth in federal spending: Impose a statutory cap limiting the annual growth in total federal spending to the sum of the inflation rate plus the percentage of population growth. (56.57%).

7. *Defund, Repeal, & Replace Government-run Health Care*

Repeal the health care legislation: Defund, repeal and replace the Patient Protection and Affordable Care Act. (56.39%).

8. *Pass an 'All-of-the-Above" Energy Policy*

Pass an 'All-of-the-Above' Energy Policy: Authorize the exploration of additional energy reserves to reduce American dependence on foreign energy sources and reduce regulatory barriers to all other forms of energy creation. (55.5%).

9. *Stop the Pork*

Reduce Earmarks: Place a moratorium on all earmarks until the budget is balanced, and then require a 2/3 majority to pass any earmark. (55.47%).

10. *Stop the Tax Hikes*

> **Reduce Taxes**: Permanently repeal all recent tax increases, and extend permanently the George W. Bush temporary reductions in income tax, capital gains tax, and estate taxes, currently scheduled to end in 2011. (53.38%).

The Contract from America an interesting political document designed to rally people around a set of policies that was generated from the bottom up. It is a clarion call for those who recognize the importance of free market principles, limited government, and individual liberty. It defines a way for the Tea Party movement to bridge citizen protests with ballot box success. The Contract from America is a natural extension of a movement that began in the local communities and quickly spread across America in response to unprecedented government expansion, reckless spending, and a blatant disregard by our leaders of the nation's founding principles.

The tea party movement has gotten a lot of people off the sidelines and into the political arena. Tea Party activists are not typical protestors. They are average middle Americans worried about making ends meet, taking care of their families, and doing their jobs—most of whom never previously participated in any kid of protect. The Tea Party Movement brought together a lot of like-minded citizens who thought they were alone in the world. They realized that not only were they not alone, but there were millions of others just as concerned. The issues and advocacy within the Tea Party Movement are issues that resonate with the majority of Americans. They worry that the enemies within are transforming America in way we do not want—in unconstitutional ways.

Tea Party Patriots are citizens, taxpayers, voters—Americans.

God Bless America

God Bless America,

Land that I love.

Stand beside her, and guide her,

Through the night with the light from above.

From the mountains, to the prairies,

to the oceans, white with foam,

God Bless America,

My home sweet home.

God Bless America,

My home sweet home

God Bless America

From the mountains, to the prairies,

to the oceans, white with foam,

God Bless America,

My home sweet home.

God Bless America,

My home sweet home.

The Star Spangled Banner

Oh, say can you see by the dawn's early light
What so proudly we hailed at the twilight's last gleaming?
Whose broad stripes and bright stars thru the perilous fight,
O'er the ramparts we watched were so gallantly streaming?
And the rocket's red glare, the bombs bursting in air,
Gave proof through the night that our flag was still there.
Oh, say does that star-spangled banner yet wave
O'er the land of the free and the home of the brave?

On the shore, dimly seen through the mists of the deep,
Where the foe's haughty host in dread silence reposes,
What is that which the breeze, o'er the towering steep,
As it fitfully blows, half conceals, half discloses?
Now it catches the gleam of the morning's first beam,
In full glory reflected now shines in the stream:
'Tis the star-spangled banner! Oh long may it wave
O'er the land of the free and the home of the brave!

And where is that band who so vauntingly swore
That the havoc of war and the battle's confusion,
A home and a country should leave us no more!
Their blood has washed out their foul footsteps' pollution.
No refuge could save the hireling and slave
From the terror of flight, or the gloom of the grave:
And the star-spangled banner in triumph doth wave
O'er the land of the free and the home of the brave!

Oh! thus be it ever, when freemen shall stand
Between their loved home and the war's desolation!
Blest with victory and peace, may the heav'n rescued land
Praise the Power that hath made and preserved us a nation.
Then conquer we must, when our cause it is just,
And this be our motto: "In God is our trust."
And the star-spangled banner in triumph shall wave
O'er the land of the free and the home of the brave!

—Francis Scott Key

28

Fight for America

We have been blessed by having the great good fortune of living in the United States of America. We are among the most fortunate people of history—enjoying unparalleled liberty, opportunity and prosperity.

> *My God! How little do my countrymen know what precious blessings they are in possession of, and which no other people on earth enjoy!*
>
> —Thomas Jefferson

We have shared a dream—The American Dream

> *There are those, I know, who will say that the liberation of humanity, the freedom of man and mind, is nothing but a dream. They are right. It is the American dream.*
>
> —Archibald MacLeish

We've become complacent. We've forgotten that freedom is not free.

> *We have enjoyed so much freedom for so long that we are perhaps in danger of forgetting how much blood it cost to establish the Bill of Rights.*
>
> —Felix Frankfurte

Our politicians are embolden with power. They believeve that they know better what we need than we do. The government has gone rogue, spurning the consent of the people.

*We hold these truths to be self-evident, that all men are
created equal, that they are endowed by their Creator
with certain unalienable Rights, that among these are
Life, Liberty and the pursuit of Happiness. −That to
secure these rights, Governments are instituted among
Men, deriving their just powers from
the consent of the governed.*

—Declaration of Independence

Our freedoms are in danger. America is at risk.

*In the long history of the world, only a few generations
have been granted the role of defending freedom in
its hour of maximum danger. I do not shrink from this
responsibility−I welcome it. I do not believe that any
of us would exchange places with any other people or
any other generation. The energy, the faith, the devotion
which we bring to this endeavor will light our country
and all who serve it−and the glow from that fire can
truly light the world.*

*And so, my fellow Americans: ask not what your country
can do for you−ask what you can do for your country.*

—John F. Kennedy
Inaugural Address

What Can *You* Do For America?

What small action can you take today to help preserve our pre-
cious freedoms? America has done much for us. What can you
do, *today*, for America?

*Nobody made a greater mistake than he who did nothing
because he could only do a little.*

—Edmund Burke

The liberties of our country, the freedom of our civil Constitution, are worth defending at all hazards; and it is our duty to defend them against all attacks. We have received them as a fair inheritance from our worthy ancestors: they purchased them for us with toil and danger and expense of treasure and blood, and transmitted them to us with care and diligence. It will bring an everlasting mark of infamy on the present generation, enlightened as it is, if we should suffer them to be wrested from us by violence without a struggle, or to be cheated out of them by the artifices of false and designing men.

—Samuel Adams

Docpotter

Beverly A. Potter has authored many books packed with useful information. She holds a Masters of Science in vocational rehabilitation counseling from San Francisco State and a doctorate in counseling psychology from Stanford University. She is a corporate trainer and was a member of the staff development team at Stanford University for nearly twenty years and a member of the Goldman School of Public Policy Executive Seminars faculty. Docpotter is a dynamic and informative speaker. Her website is docpotter.com. You can also find her on Twitter, Facebook and elswhere in cyberspace. Please visit.

The Patriots Handbook is available for Tea Parties and other groups in lots of 30 at substantial discount for fund raisers. For information, contact Ronin Publishing, 510-420-3669, ronin@roninpub.com.

Count Your Blessings
and Thank America

We live in the greatest, most properous country in the history of the world. Even the poorest American is among top fifteen percent of the world's wealthiest citizens. The Founding Fathers entrusted us with this wonderful, exceptional country. What are we doing to preserve and protect her? What are *you* doing?